Endorsements for

Balanced Leadership In Unbalanced Times

"Rob Pasick reminds all leaders and aspiring leaders ... that from deep self-awareness come action and fulfillment."

—Thomas Glocer, CEO, Thomson Reuters

"... A treasure chest of advice on how to get centered and live meaningfully."

—Robert E. Quinn, author and professor, Univ. of Michigan Ross School of Business

D1568031

"The book is chock-full of helpful tools ..."

—Jane Dutton, professor, U-M Ross School of Business and co-director, Center for Positive Organizational Scholarship

"Rob's book explains the importance of achieving balance and provides a clear set of guidelines."

—James Ratner, executive vice president, Forest City Enterprises and chairman and CEO, Forest City Commercial Group

"This book is applicable and inspiring for people at all levels. It is an approach to developing and growing leadership skills that I found both useful and practical."

—Elizabeth Ross, president and chief marketing officer, Tribal DDB Worldwide

"A quick read with thorough and practical suggestions that can be applied to your personal and professional life."

—Bill Hermann, CPA, managing partner, Plante & Moran

"... Easy ideas to incorporate into your leadership style."

—Bruce Baumbach, plant manager, Global
Engine Manufacturing Alliance

"Rob gives us the formula of awareness to guide ourselves and others through turbulent and challenging times with sustained energy."

—Eddie Erlandson, M.D., executive coach, leadership consultant and executive vice president, Worth Ethic Corp.

"Passion and balance are indeed critical to success."

—Ted Dacko, president and CEO, HealthMedia Inc.

"The perfect book to throw in the bag and take on all trips."

—Joshua Pokempner, owner, Giddy Up! Publishing

"... A host of very practical guidelines for achieving balance and effectiveness in life and in leadership. You will be nodding your head in agreement."

—Kim Cameron, William Russell Kelly professor,
U-M Ross School of Business

"What I found most unique and helpful was the core tool within the book, the Coach's Clipboard."

—David Meitz, managing director, Investment
   Technology Group Inc.

"Rob Pasick implores us to model leadership by practicing mindfulness as we search out balance in our lives and return daily to redefining success and contentment."

—David S. Ufer, president, Ufer & Co. Insurance

"Rob's book is a must-read as you try to balance the many demands that leaders face in our fast-paced world."

—Larry Freed, president and CEO, ForeSee Results

"Rob Pasick reminds us that good leadership is based on the timeless principles of integrity, acceptance and compassion toward others and ourselves."

—Farida Ali, CEO, Dynamic Computer

"Pasick reminds us that our core values are based on simple principles. We just have to make the effort to know what they are."

—Dr. David Canter, director, Healthcare Strategy Initiative,
   William Davidson Institute, University of Michigan

"An outstanding guide for leadership and personal success. I found every page had something useful or inspirational for me to learn from."

—Paul Freedman, president, LimnoTech

"Read Rob Pasick's *Balanced Leadership in Unbalanced Times* and learn how to ease balance into your life one step at a time."

—Marshall Goldsmith, executive coach and best-selling author of *What Got You Here Won't Get You There*

"I found jewels in this book that I will share with my team, even my kids, but mostly that I can use to lead in the best way I can."

—Dan Mulhern, author, radio host and First Gentleman of the State of Michigan

"Rob uses his vast experience as a personal counselor and leadership consultant to create a set of simple but important guidelines on how to create … balance."

—Frank Ascione, dean, University of Michigan School of Pharmacy

"Inside … you will find the fundamentals for achieving effective leadership and especially a balanced and accomplished life."

—Miguel A. Vicente, CEO, Grupo Antolin North America Inc.

"Dr. Rob Pasick's new book is … a powerful tool to help you succeed in the business of life."

—Lucy Ann Lance, host of The Lucy Ann Lance Show, WLBY-AM (1290)

"Rob Pasick helps us go beyond understanding what matters to helping us know how to make use of that understanding."

—Bill Upton, CEO, Malloy Publishers

"The book convincingly makes the case for a life of passion and balance while providing a recipe for doing so."

—Chuck Newman, CEO, ReCellular Inc.

"This book is a true how-to manual for becoming your absolute best."

—Gino Wickman, author of *Traction: Get a Grip on Your Business*

Robert Pasick

BALANCED LEADERSHIP
IN UNBALANCED TIMES

ROBERT PASICK, PH.D.
WITH KATHLEEN O'GORMAN

For ongoing discussion and additional material, visit

www.RobsLeaders.info

You may contact the author at
RobsLeaders@gmail.com

Cover art and design by
Rick Nease
www.RickNease.com

Published by
David Crumm Media, LLC
42015 Ford Rd., Suite 234
Canton, Michigan 48187
U.S.A.

For information about customized editions, bulk purchases or
permissions, contact David Crumm Media, LLC at
info@DavidCrummMedia.com
734-786-3815
www.RobsLeaders.info

Contents

Introduction: Righting the Ship

T he aspiring leaders I've worked with for some three decades have taught me many things, but these are two of the most important:

- Great leaders constantly strive to strike a balance between work and the other realms of their lives.
- Great leaders share a passion: They want to make a difference in the world.

Here's something else I've learned along the way: Those two things go hand in hand. The most successful leaders are the ones who work the hardest at balancing all aspects of their lives. And when they do, they find that they really do make a difference.

It sounds way too simple, doesn't it? The truth is, achieving balance isn't simple or easy. It takes a whole lot of effort, especially during times like these when companies—and indeed whole countries—are thrown into turmoil.

For the second time in this young century, America faces a daunting challenge. The first came with the utter shock and horror of the Sept. 11, 2001, terrorist attacks. The second rumbled up with the economic earthquakes that began rattling the world in 2008. This new crisis not only threatened to engulf thousands more than the earlier one, but it was poised to test the mettle of leaders around the globe in ways not seen for decades.

Could the people at the top handle the stress? Would they have the talent, wisdom and fortitude to keep the rest of us focused and engaged, even as we worried about losing our shirts along with our jobs?

The best leaders look at the cold, hard facts, make a plan and march forward. People want and need to know that leaders are, in fact, leading, not panicking or cowering in fear.

Few of us are in a position to alter world events as a government treasury chief—or a new American president—is able to do. Nudged by the global financial crisis, however, we can look with fresh eyes at what really matters in our own world. Now more than ever, it seems clear that if we pay closer attention to our families, our communities and our personal well-being as well as our jobs, we'll not only be better leaders but better people. This seems to be one of the clear messages of the 2008 presidential election.

With that in mind, I will offer in these pages dozens of ideas on how you can boost your ability to balance your life. Begin with my 20-point mental checklist on what makes a balanced leader. Then I'll walk you through concepts that I use in my work as a clinical and organizational psychologist and executive coach. At the end of the book, you'll find other resources and an invitation to join me online at RobsLeaders.info. It's the place where I hope we can keep the conversation going.

What Do I Mean By Balanced Leadership?

Here are 20 principles that I think define a balanced leader:

1. You balance your needs with those of others in your organization.
2. You balance your needs with those of others in your family.
3. You manage your energy.
4. You manage your time.
5. You adhere to your values.

6. You keep an optimistic outlook while remaining realistic.

7. You cultivate consistency while adapting to change.

8. You practice self-reflection.

9. You maintain your emotional equanimity.

10. You recognize and manage your blind spots.

11. You leverage your strengths while managing your weaknesses.

12. You try to see yourself as others see you.

13. You alternate periods of hard work with periods of sustained rest.

14. You play as hard as you work.

15. You take chances and make mistakes.

16. You acknowledge your mistakes.

17. You learn from your mistakes.

18. You maintain a good sense of humor.

19. You cultivate friends and relatives to keep you on the right path.

20. You never do any of this alone.

In unbalanced times, it's more important than ever to practice these principles. The mark of a good leader is the ability to lead in all kinds of circumstances. In the toughest of times, leaders need to stand on a rock-solid set of core values.

Remember—life almost always is unbalanced, out of kilter, listing or leaning in one direction or another. No matter what, you'll need the skills and strength to help you steady the ship.

CHAPTER 1

Thank God It's Friday

As a leadership coach, I haven't been immune from the struggle to live a balanced life, but my wife, Pat, and I were lucky when our children were young. As clinical psychologists, we could set our own schedules. The one drawback was that we had to work nights because we were family therapists and often saw clients in the evening.

To accommodate both of our needs, we came up with an arrangement where one of us would be home after school almost every day to take care of our two sons and the household. I worked Tuesday and Thursday nights, and Pat worked Monday and Wednesday nights. When one of us was working, the other usually would take over when the kids got out of school. In addition, when the kids were preschoolers, I often took Fridays off to do things with them. This arrangement gave us a good balance between our work and home lives. It actually was a very gratifying time for both of us. While Pat continued to shoulder most of the household and child-care responsibilities, I was able to be more involved in the care of the boys than most of the men I knew.

I like to tell the story of when my oldest son Adam, who is now in his 30s, was going off to college and I took him out for a good-bye breakfast. He told me how great it was to have the breakfast, especially since it was on a Friday. I didn't know what he was talking about and said something like, "Yeah, Friday's a great day—TGIF." And he said, "I don't think you get it, Dad. I like Fridays with you because I remember when I was just a preschooler and you'd be home on Fridays. I always looked forward to that. There were two things I loved about Fridays— one was that you were home and the other was that the Muppets were on."

To hear that was like winning Olympic gold, but there is another side to my story.

When Oprah Calls

When the kids were teenagers, I got really caught up in writing books, and I had a fair degree of success. I began to act as though my time was more important than my wife's or my children's. I was obsessed with traveling and giving workshops and what my next book was going to be.

I'd published a book—*Awakening from the Deep Sleep*— about men and their relationships and how they should live their lives differently. And the book was very well received.

That spring, we'd scheduled a family vacation to Hilton Head Island. My cousins were joining us, too. But three days into the trip, my assistant called to say, "You got a call from Oprah. They have an opening on the show and they want you to be on it." But the opening was just two days away—in the middle of our vacation.

Without hesitating or consulting my family, I made arrangements to go to Chicago. Later, I told my wife how excited I was. She was gracious about my leaving, even helping me buy a new suit to wear on the show, but I didn't think about the fact that I was leaving her alone with the kids and my cousins.

It wasn't until I returned a few days later that it dawned on me: I was so caught up in my success that I had put my own need for fame ahead of the family's need for my time.

I'd done a lot of things in my life, but the fact that I was on *The Oprah Winfrey Show* was special. People started calling me "Oprah Man" and asking me what Oprah was like. I'm not ashamed to admit that it went straight to my head. I was seduced by success. It was amazing how easy it was for me to set aside some of my basic values. And the irony of it, of course, was that my book was about how men should shed their self-centered behavior. I was becoming a case study for my own book!

It took a while, but eventually I came to my senses. The demands of family and daily life forced me to reset my priorities. One result was that I didn't write another book for several years, due in large part to the realization that it was time for me to back off.

Tuning Out To Tune In

My children are grown now and on their own, and I've moved from family therapy to leadership coaching. If anything, I'm busier than ever, but even though my circumstances have changed, I still have to work hard at the business of balancing my life.

I've employed many techniques in the struggle and advocated many more to my clients. You'll read about them in the pages ahead. But one of the easiest things anyone can do—and something that has helped me tremendously over the years—is to take a time-out in the form of meditation. I taught myself the technique when I was 21 years old, and now I can tune out the world in a millisecond. If I have a 10-minute break, I can close my eyes and instantly be in an altered state.

I especially like to do this when I feel that midday slump coming on, around 3 or 4 o'clock. I can do it in the office or sitting in my car, but my favorite place to do it is on the porch, hearing the birds sing and leaves rustle. It's amazing how energized I feel afterward. And it's a reminder that sometimes the simplest acts can restore the spirit. I encourage anyone who is feeling out of sync to find a technique like this that will help "pause" the day and replenish the soul.

Another thing that helps to keep me balanced is having my responsibilities at home clearly defined. Otherwise, it might be easy for me to say that I'm too busy to unload the dishwasher or fix breakfast. It's not as if I have a lot of duties, but I have enough that I can't pull rank and say my work is so important that I can't do my part.

Leaving Footprints

More and more business executives are looking for tools to help them deal with the ever-increasing demands on their time and energy. Like most of us, they're trying to keep four or five balls in the air—and living in fear that if they drop one, all will come tumbling down.

Americans don't have a good track record on juggling. Traditionally, we've focused too much on work while ignoring the fact that if we drop that ball—if we lose our job or go through major difficulties or disruptions in the workplace— we'll likely recover in time, even though it may not seem like it at first. We forget that if we drop the ball at home or in other areas of our lives, we may not bounce back so easily.

Neglecting a marriage can lead to divorce and long-lasting heartache. Not paying attention to our kids can send them into a tailspin. If we pull back from friendships or our larger community, we risk triggering depression and loneliness. Disregarding our health—mental or physical—can have dire and irreversible consequences. If we violate our personal values, we risk losing the respect of others, and even ourselves, possibly forever.

Despite our propensity to pour more time and energy into work, our culture is changing. People in every generation, from baby boomers to millennials, are seeking the keys to a life of greater meaning. They want their values to permeate everything, from work to home life and free time.

Shifting economic forces and strident cultural wars are helping to spur these changes. There's no longer a mentality of abundance, of an unbounded world and resources without end. People are tired of the endless fighting over beliefs. As information rockets around the globe at warp speed, people are more aware than ever that their actions can have wide impact—

and that they might have less control over what the impact might be. The result is a deep desire to reset the balance, to restore meaning, to find personal points of balance.

You've probably heard the term "carbon footprint." It's a way to measure the impact of humans on the environment in terms of the production of greenhouse gases like carbon dioxide. Well, people also are worrying more and more about their personal footprints. They're asking, "What will I leave behind? Will anyone notice that I have passed this way?"

The popularity of the last lecture of Randy Pausch, the Carnegie Mellon University computer science professor who died of pancreatic cancer, is a case in point. Millions of people have been drawn to his story through the video of his lecture on YouTube and his best-selling book with Jeffrey Zaslow, *The Last Lecture*. Why? People are inspired by a life not lived in vain.

The desire to leave something behind is deeply ingrained. But we don't have to literally change the world to leave a powerful legacy. If you read any of the *Portraits of Grief* in the New York Times—the short profiles of those who died in the Sept. 11, 2001, terrorist attacks on the World Trade Center—you saw that some of the most vivid memories about the victims were tied to ordinary, everyday experiences.

CHAPTER 2

Establishing Your Balance Points

L ike everyone else, business leaders want to have an impact—and not only at work. They realize it's not enough just to have a title on the door. They want to have influence in civic life or in a faith-based or social network or movement. They want time to take care of their bodies and their souls, and they don't want to be strangers in their own homes. The challenge is to find a way, every day, to balance these arenas, even in small ways.

Sometimes, for example, leaders make the mistake of thinking they can lead at home as they do at work. But different settings call for different styles. At home, leadership, of necessity, becomes much more collaborative. You can't disengage as you walk in the door, but you also can't be "the boss." You must operate within a partnership framework.

No matter what the setting, it's important for leaders to be in tune with those around them. You can't be a lone wolf. You can't do it all by yourself. If you try to operate without the support of the pack, you're not likely to survive. This is especially relevant for today's two-career families, where it's harder than ever to keep the home fires burning. Research shows that women still carry more than their fair share of the responsibility for child care, taking care of the extended family and handling household duties.

The most effective leaders are multidimensional. They're not pedal-to-the-metal types who do nothing but work for the bottom line. They're energetic and driven, but they're able to shift nimbly from one arena to the next—and that helps to establish balance points. They work intensely, and they rest intensely. They get things accomplished, but they don't expend all of their energy in one area to the detriment of others. And they don't try to do everything at once. They may not balance out every day, but they do it over time.

Ways To Ease The Way

E.B. White said, "I arise in the morning torn between a desire to improve (or save) the world and a desire to enjoy (or savor) the world. This makes it hard to plan the day."

Like White, we get out of bed every day facing a host of choices. There is no one-size-fits-all formula for how we order the day or lead our lives. Each of us must decide what will sustain us, taking into account our energy, values and passions.

Here are examples of what successful leaders do to buoy themselves as they search for balance.

Developing routines and practices can help with life's transitions and prevent becoming overwhelmed by competing demands and desires.

- Real estate developer Peter Allen starts his day with a glass of fresh-squeezed orange juice, online reading of more than a half-dozen newspapers plus the home-delivered New York Times, a special mix of five kinds of cereals with fruit and yogurt and "lots of thinking." That sets the tone. "After a day at the office," he says, "I still have the energy to teach a class, play golf or tennis or have a wonderful time with the grandkids."

- John Baldoni, a leadership consultant and coach, uses his morning exercise routine to think about what lies ahead for the day. "Running regularly, coupled with lifting weights, gives me the energy I need to think critically as well as creatively," he says. "I also augment my fitness regimen with golf, which I often play by myself. Walking the course gives me plenty of time to think and reflect and in the process gain insight into the challenges of the day."

- Yoga practice helps Bob Galardi, an executive coach, not only relieve pain and sore muscles but control stress. He uses calm-inducing yoga breathing before heading into a stressful situation.

Integrating home and work schedules can keep one or the other from tipping into the danger zone.

- "I enter all the kids' schedules (soccer, swimming, school plays etc.) into my work calendar and make a point to schedule travel and other meetings so that I can attend at least two or three events per week—even if that event is picking them up from practice," says Kit Dickinson, president of an information technology company. "The car rides home are a great opportunity to connect with the child and hear how their day went or anything else they want to talk about."

Being realistic and accepting the obvious—that juggling life and work can be messy—can save a lot of worry and heartache.

- "There are always times when work projects overwhelm life and life responsibilities trump work. The only way to avoid these balance swings is to either not have a life or not have to work," says Marisa Smith, an entrepreneur and partner in an information technology company. "Since neither of these is an option for us, we prefer to be realistic about the fact that there will be days when things will be out of whack. Managing our own expectations helps keep our frustration levels lower and enables us to maintain perspective until the pendulum swings back in the other direction."

Taking small steps can lead to big results.

- Planning guru Alan Lakein, author of *How to Get Control of Your Time and Life*, advocates using a five-minute rule if you can't seem to get started on a project. Set a timer for five minutes and work on the project. When the timer goes off, move on to something else or set the timer for another five minutes. Most people keep going for much longer than five minutes.

- I counsel clients to identify the time of day when they do their most creative work, then to keep that time free of meetings and distractions.

Asking questions can turn up surprisingly helpful answers.

- Rick Reid, an account development manager for an office furniture company, advises having the courage to ask others in your life—spouse, coworkers and friends—how you are doing as a husband, colleague and friend. "It can produce powerful revelations and the possibility of change that can bring about better balance overall," Rick says.

- Deborah Orlowski, an internal consultant for a university, was amazed when one of her clients seemed to heal so quickly after her husband's death at a young age. "I asked her how she did it, and she said, 'We never left anything undone. When we were angry, we fought and got over it. We told each other we loved each other. We played together. We shared. Sure, I would have loved more time with him, but I have no regrets because there is no guilt … Nothing was left undone.' " That conversation changed Deborah's life. Now, she strives not to leave anything important undone or unsaid.

Looking more closely at what's driving your bus can help you steer a little better.

- As Rick Reid says: "We are driven in our culture to succeed and to have more. I am just coming to grips with this in the past few years in my own life. How many others are also—those with 3,500-square-foot homes and Hummers in the driveway? How many really get that 'less is more'? ... If our society were not driven by the constant accumulation of money, how might that change the way we live? I like money and enjoy what I can do with it, but it does not rule me."

Teamwork Works

A big step on the way to a more balanced life is assembling the best leadership team. This requires recognition that it really isn't all about you. If the members of your team are talented and trustworthy, they will be effective, and you will be able to delegate with confidence. You'll be free to do the things you are exceptional at, and you will have more free time—capital that you can spend as you like.

I like the advice that I heard Hall of Famer Joe Dumars, president of basketball operations for the Detroit Pistons, give during a talk at the University of Michigan in which he stressed that, for him, the most important aspect of team building is to pick people of the highest character. Be very selective, Dumars advised, and surround yourself with the right people.

As you do that, it's important to resist the urge to tap clones of yourself. Select people who are strong in different ways and who can complement one another. If you're the creative, big-picture type, make sure someone on your team is better at the gritty details. If you're highly competitive but tend to rub people the wrong way, pick someone who is great at schmoozing and not as highly charged. Each member of the team should play off the strengths—and weaknesses—of others.

Once you have a great team, let everyone do their job. That's what the team is there for. You won't be forced to do things you're not very good at or qualified to do. The team will step up. One of my clients put together a very strong team as he built his company. When he was ready to expand, he was able to turn his full attention to his mission while his team kept things humming internally.

Recognizing the importance of your team also will give you the proper perspective on yourself. Otherwise, you may think that you can solve everything. Failing to recognize your limits can be your undoing. Working with a team will keep an overinflated sense of how powerful and important you are from taking over.

This point was brought home to me by Robert Chapman, president and CEO of United Bancorp Inc., based in Michigan. "Leaders may be powerful and extremely important to their companies, but they're also just ordinary people—no better or worse than anyone else," Bob notes. "If your company or department or project is successful, it's not just because of you—it's because everyone has done their job, including the cleaning crews who came in after you went home at night."

CHAPTER 3

Discovering Your Strengths

Everyone has a unique set of strengths and abilities, and the more time you spend using these unique talents, the more successful and satisfied you're likely to be. I often employ several methods to get my clients to come to a deeper understanding of their talents.

One of the easiest methods—and one I've turned to many times—was developed by Dan Sullivan, author and founder of *Strategic Coach*, who advocates simply sending e-mails to the people who know you best. Explain that you're going through a leadership development process and ask them to describe your unique strengths, talents and contributions.

I've found that the responses people get are pretty consistent. It shouldn't be too surprising because, for most of us, certain threads weave through our lives. Back in grade school, if you were always organizing neighborhood games or teams, chances are you're still doing it in some fashion at 20, 30, 40 or 50.

Another great tool is the Internet-based StrengthsFinder Profile, created by Donald O. Clifton, Tom Rath and a team of scientists from the Gallup Organization. It was later renamed the Clifton StrengthsFinder, and a new Web site and book,

StrengthsFinder 2.0, were published in 2007. When you buy the book, you get an access code so you can take the assessment online. The program analyzes your answers and comes up with the five most powerful signature themes you display. Based on that, you receive action plans and other activities designed to help you understand how best to use your strengths. Here's where to find out more: www.strengthsfinder.com.

A similar exercise was developed by my colleagues at the Center for Positive Organizational Scholarship at the University of Michigan's Ross School of Business. As with Sullivan's approach, you request positive feedback from people who know you and then use this information to create a portrait of your "best self." You can find out more about the Reflected Best Self Exercise at www.bus.umich.edu/Positive/POS-Teaching-and-Learning/ReflectedBestSelfExercise.htm.

After using one of these methods, I usually counsel my clients to work with the top five strengths they've identified. It's a comfortable number for goal setting.

Another helpful tool is the Denison Organizational Culture Survey. It's an online survey designed to look at an organization's culture and performance and to measure progress toward achieving results. Employees are surveyed anonymously and the responses are tabulated and translated into a profile that compares the organization to characteristics from a database of others from around the world. You can learn more about the survey at www.denisonconsulting.com.

Draft A Personal Mission Statement

Mission is about a very big question: What are you here on Earth to do?

It's a question most of us ponder at some point in our lives, but it's one of the most difficult to answer. Surprisingly, many successful leaders do have an answer, and in the best cases there is strong alignment between what they are leading and what they perceive as their mission.

When I think of mission, I think of action:

- I am here **to do** something.
- I am here **to act** on the environment.

A mission is usually so big, it's rarely finished. It's not necessarily a goal to be achieved but more like a lifelong journey with an ending off in the distant future. It also isn't something you invent. More than likely, it's something that springs from deep inside, something you've been doing or an inclination you've had all along.

My mission is to make the world a better place by helping individuals and organizations reach their full potential. That sounds vague and immeasurable. Yet, for as long as I can remember, this is what I have been all about. It was my mission even before I could conceptualize the notion of a mission.

When there was racial tension in the high school I attended, I organized other students and we put together a student relations council to talk about and deal with the problems. That ability to bring people of different backgrounds together is something I've been dedicated to my whole life. I'm not sure where it came from, but it has always been part of my mission.

As you get ready to draft your personal mission statement, ask yourself:

- What are the things that have driven me since I was a young adult?
- What decisions have I made tied to these impulses— things that I've done and things that I've decided *not* to do?
- What actions have I taken to further my mission?

Describe Your Vision Of Success

Ari Weinzweig, cofounder of the famous Zingerman's Deli in Ann Arbor, Mich., has one of the best approaches to formulating a vision that I've seen. He believes that while an organization's mission and vision should be compatible, they aren't the same. In his view, a mission is global in scope and never-ending. A vision is a mental picture of success, time-constrained, inspiring and specific enough that it can be measured.

To figure out your vision, Weinzweig advises answering this question:

When you're really successful at a point in the future, what will that success look like?

As you try to peer into the future, consider these factors:

- Employ sensory-based images: What would success physically look like? What would it feel like?

- Be specific: How many people will there be in your organization? Where is it located? How big will your family be? Where will you live?

- Let your vision inspire. It should get your juices flowing.

These are among the reasons Weinzweig offers for the need to create a vision:

- It has a positive impact on others.

- It attracts good people.

- It allows us to create reality instead of just reacting to present-day problems.

- It's a statement of optimism in the future.

- It forces us to act on and model the reality that there is no safe path.

- It forces us to hold ourselves accountable.

- It tells us what we aren't going to do.

- It tells everyone what's in it for them.

- It creates positive movement within the organization.

- It helps keep good people.

Once you have your vision, Weinzweig says you should write it down and, of course, communicate it to others. But beyond simply communicating it, he says you have to "sell" it—talk it up, display it, promote it and otherwise make it an integral part of your culture.

Define Your Core Values

These are the things you stick with no matter what. They may be as simple as, "I'm always going to tell the truth" or "I'm always going to respect others." They are the principles you abide by and vow not to compromise, knowing that sooner or later you will be in situations where a course of action isn't clear. These values will guide your actions.

Your list of core values should include statements about what you will and will not do in conducting your life. They serve as a guide to your decision-making and attitude formation. Without core values as a guide, it is easy to lose your way personally and professionally.

Here are some examples of individual core values:

- Stay true to my faith.
- Show the love I have for the people in my life.
- Encourage people to succeed at their highest values.
- Set the right values for my company and my family, and adhere to them.
- Always tell the truth, no matter how difficult.
- Never inflict physical or emotional violence on another human being.
- Recognize the good in others.
- Always uphold my sense of integrity and adhere to my ethics.

Oprah Winfrey captured it all with these words: "Real integrity is doing the right thing, knowing that nobody's going to know whether you did it or not."

Challenge Your Irrational Ideas

Many of life's problems stem not so much from the things that happen to us as from how we interpret these events. Whether we realize it or not, most of us carry around one or more irrational ideas that act as filters for our experiences. These may cause us to react more strongly and inappropriately to events than is warranted.

In his research, psychologist Albert Ellis identified a famous "dirty dozen" of these irrational ideas. See if you recognize yourself in any of them:

1. Adults must be loved by significant others for almost everything they do.
2. Certain acts are awful or wicked, and the people who perform them should be damned.
3. It's horrible when things are not the way we like them to be.
4. Human misery is invariably externally caused and forced on us by outside people and events.
5. If something is or may be dangerous or fearsome, we should be terribly upset and obsess about it endlessly.
6. It's easier to avoid than to face life's difficulties and responsibilities.
7. We absolutely need something or someone stronger or greater than ourselves on which to rely.
8. We should be thoroughly competent, intelligent and achieving in all possible respects.
9. Because something once strongly affected our life, it should indefinitely affect it.
10. We must have certain and perfect control over things.
11. Human happiness can be achieved by inertia and inaction.
12. We have virtually no control over our emotions and cannot help feeling disturbed about things.

Once you learn to recognize your irrational baggage, you can challenge those assumptions as they arise—and close the lid on them.

CHAPTER 4

Scoping Out Your Goals

When I work with business leaders, I often use an exercise, a precursor to setting goals, that helps them zero in on areas needing work. The exercise goes like this:

1. Imagine that you are at the center of a personal ecosystem.

2. Swirling around you are five circles, symbols of the main spheres of influence in your life.

Your Personal Ecosystem: The 5 Key Spheres of Life

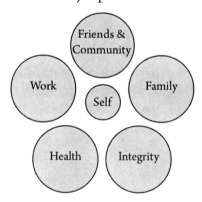

Now, draw a line from the "Self" in the middle to each of the spheres.

If the relationship is strong and there are no major issues, draw a solid line:

_____

If the relationship is strained in some way, or you feel there is unfinished business or some minor problem, draw a dotted line:

— — — — — —

If the relationship has a serious problem, draw a jagged line:

∿∿∿∿∿

Men and women tend to focus on different circles. For women, it's often the conflict between their roles as leaders at work and as wives and mothers at home. As Michelle Obama told an audience on the 2008 presidential campaign trail, her husband, Barack, "has seen me worry that when I'm at work, I'm not spending enough time with the kids. And when I'm with the kids, I'm not spending enough time at work. Never feeling like I'm doing anything right—always feeling just a little guilty."

For men, a common problem is feeling as if they're not achieving enough at work. As one of my clients put it, "No matter how hard I work, I never seem to be able to keep up. If I'm doing one thing, I am constantly interrupted by my BlackBerry or by a hundred email messages in an hour or by text messages. The faster I go, the further behind I get ... I fear that this all will come crashing in on me someday. I know I should also be attending to my health, but I have no time to exercise or eat well."

When people do this exercise honestly, they can quickly pinpoint areas where they have tension and stress. The next step is to set goals and an action plan to address the problems.

In one case, a man who was estranged from his son initially refused to take the first step to patch things up. But once he realized that waiting for the son to contact him wasn't going to work, he decided to take the initiative. He realized that he probably owed his son an apology and that would go a long way toward drawing them back together.

In another instance, a man who was both overweight and a smoker used many excuses to avoid dealing with his problems. He couldn't stop smoking because he feared he'd gain more weight, and he couldn't exercise because the effects of smoking would leave him winded. To break the do-nothing cycle, I suggested he first consult a doctor. He finally did and discovered there was medication that could help him quit smoking. He'd taken his first step toward overcoming his problems.

Almost anything can be resolved if you isolate the problem and set a course of action. Acting will make you feel better immediately. But if you remain in denial and do nothing, chances are the problem will eat away at you.

Be Realistic

It's important to be realistic when you set goals—to pick things that you have some reasonable expectation and probability of achieving. You don't want to set a goal of playing basketball in the NBA when you didn't even make your high school team.

Goals also should be specific and measurable. Don't figure on changing your personality or something fundamental about you; rather, it's about altering your behavior so you can reach the goal. So, focus on things that you can control. (Realize, too, that you can't control someone else's behavior, though you can control your reaction to what they do.)

The Serenity Prayer is useful to keep in mind as you set goals. What are you hoping or praying for? Are you seeking the courage to set a goal or should you be aiming for something short of that—a "serenity goal" of acceptance and the courage to deal with a problem or issue on that level?

Break down your goals into achievable steps. Your goal may be to quit smoking. But the first step might be to limit the number of cigarettes you smoke in a day. Then you might restrict the places where you smoke them. Each step should take you closer to your ultimate goal.

And finally, when you do succeed at one of your goals, enjoy your success. Reward yourself. Buy something you've wanted. Take a trip you've been meaning to take. Do something that gives you a pat on the back and brings a smile to your face.

Commit To Action

For most of my life, I've used a simple goal-setting method that I learned from a colleague as a young man. I write my goals on index cards using this format:

- **What?** The specific, measurable goals that I want to achieve and the date that I set them. (No vague dreams.)
- **By when?** The date for achieving the goals. (Research shows that 90-day goals can be most effective. Longer-term ones tend to get lost; shorter-term ones come to resemble to-do lists.)
- **Why?** The reason why each goal is important. What values are central to the goals?
- **How?** The process, step by step, that I will use to achieve each goal.
- **Support?** The people I will work with to achieve each goal.

I have a whole box of goal cards going back to 1968. I like this system because it's intuitive. It follows the questions your brain would naturally ask: What do I want to do? How fast am I going to get it done? Why do I want to do it? How will I get it done? Who will help me?

Your plan doesn't have to be hugely detailed, but you do need a plan. As a reminder of the goals I've set, I carry a folded-up index card in my wallet listing them. I add and cross off as I go.

There are more detailed goal-setting approaches that I use with clients, but this low-tech version is easy and effective. And it's easily adaptable to our microchip-driven world. Feel free to make your shoebox full of goals a digital one.

Pick Your Support Team

One of the myths that people often hold dear is that they are responsible for their own success. But today, there is more and more acceptance of the notion that if you are going to succeed, it will be within a community, a group of other committed souls.

We shouldn't be surprised at this. Think about the great innovators and doers in history. Were they operating solo? Was Thomas Edison working alone in his lab? Was Michelangelo up on the scaffolding all by himself, day in and day out?

People seek out and rely on social connections to a far greater extent than they did even a few decades ago. Think about the success of online networking sites like LinkedIn and Facebook. If you accept that most things are accomplished with a "posse," it's clear that you must think about who will accompany you on your journey, who will support you and help fill in the gaps. This takes on even greater importance during bad economic times. If you lose your job, your network might help you find a new one. Isolated people have a much harder time of it. (And your network needn't just be online. Yours might be your bowling league or your investment club or those you worship with.)

Draw In Your Family

Business leaders have a tendency to pay meticulous attention to setting up their leadership team at work and then drop the ball at home. But families are enterprises, too.

I was struck by that fact once more after reading a story in the New York Times about Arizona Cardinals quarterback Kurt Warner and his family, which includes his wife, Brenda, and seven children. Clearly, keeping the Warner crew in line and headed in the right direction takes a lot of ingenuity and determination.

Two of the Warner children wrote down for the newspaper the *Eight Rules for Being a Warner Daughter or Son*. What they came up with is kind of a kid-friendly family mission statement, with a bit of whimsy thrown in:

1. Everyone has to agree on which strangers' meal to pay for when dining at a restaurant. [The Warners do this anonymously as a way of sharing their good fortune. –Ed.]
2. At dinner, share the favorite part of your day.
3. Hold hands and pray before every meal.
4. After ordering at a restaurant, be able to tell mom the server's eye color.
5. Throw away your trash at the movie theater and stack plates for the server at restaurants.
6. Spend one hour at an art museum when on the road.
7. Hold hands with a sibling for 10 minutes if you can't get along.
8. If you can't get along holding hands, sit cheek to cheek. (If you can't get along cheek to cheek, then it's lips to lips!)

Reading the list, you can see exactly what the Warners are about and the values they hold dear. The Warners inspired me to dig out a sheet that my wife and I put together years ago when we were family therapists. It's titled, "Some Keys to a Happy and Loving Relationship."

Here's what we wrote:

1. Learn to regularly devote time and energy to the relationship. Great relationships require high maintenance. Learning to talk productively to each other about the relationship is key to its survival. Learn the power of being present.
2. Learn to have productive disagreements. Avoid hitting below the belt. Learn how to stay calm. Avoid the blame game.

3. Be positive. Learn to reintroduce praise and admiration into your relationship. Take responsibility and learn to apologize when you may have been wrong.
4. Men: Avoid the "fix it" syndrome. Learn to just sit and listen.

Feel free to borrow from our list and add to it. The main point is that you can use mechanisms like these with your own family. Hold a family roundtable to discuss what everyone thinks should be the family's mission, vision, values and house rules. Talk over with your mate the points in our "Keys to a Happy and Loving Relationship." Team-building isn't something that you should leave behind when you shut the office door behind you.

Boost Your Resiliency Quotient

Resiliency is the ability to rebound from hardship, difficulty and misfortune and successfully adapt to adverse situations. It's perhaps more important today than ever, because the world is more interconnected than at any time in history. The "flattening of the world," as Thomas Friedman refers to it, means we experience turmoil faster, more intensely and more often. The worldwide financial turmoil of 2008 is a perfect example of that.

Nothing great in life is ever achieved without taking considerable risk and facing distinct difficulties. So, going forward, it's important to understand how you have handled adversity in the past. That's the best predictor of how you will handle it in the future.

Here are some questions to consider:
1. How accurately do you assess the risks in challenging situations?
2. Where would you place yourself on the cautiousness scale—over or under?
3. Do you tend to be excessively optimistic or pessimistic?
4. Does risk cause you to charge forward or retreat?
5. Do you set realistic but challenging goals?

Here are some resiliency-boosting strategies for tough times:

1. Carefully decide what you can control and what you can't. Focus your energy on the former.
2. Keep your perspective on your ultimate goal—for example, to save as many jobs as possible, to ensure the company's survival, to raise sensitive children, to have a happy marriage.
3. Remember, there are always other solutions. Find ways to improvise and stay flexible.
4. Avoid succumbing to temptations to quit, to cheat, to exploit.
5. Keep yourself inspired: read, discuss, pray; do whatever it takes.
6. Look for humor, even when the situation looks bleak.
7. Remember and honor your personal stories of overcoming adversity.
8. Find time to take care of yourself on a daily basis.
9. Acknowledge fear but find a way to tame it.
10. Make the tough decisions and do not look back.
11. Commit to overcoming adversity—to win and not to allow yourself to fail.
12. Be realistically optimistic but stay grounded in reality.
13. Accept responsibility for past failure but do not beat yourself up over it.
14. Find a small group of people who are willing and able to support you.
15. Cast off negative people.
16. Define specific, winnable goals.
17. Communicate the facts, no matter how bleak.

CHAPTER 5

The Coach's Clipboard

W hen I set out to write this book, my goal was to focus on principles and strategies that I use to help leaders work toward their goals while not losing sight of other important aspects of their lives.

In this chapter, you'll find a year's worth of leadership principles—collectively "The Coach's Clipboard"—that draw on real-life examples from my work and life. Accompanying each is "The Playbook"—suggestions for action, discussion points and ideas that you can employ and adapt as you like. I've left room, too, for you to figure out your own "Personal Playbook."

Not everyone will find each one of these things useful. Not everyone needs to run out and tackle every single point. Pick and choose the ones that you think will help you the most.

My coaching style is very collaborative. If I find something useful when working with a client, I can't wait to pass it along. So, much of what you will read in this chapter is based on what I've observed and learned from others. It also draws on what I've learned from the writings and research of some of the best minds in the business world—people like Robert E. Quinn, Jane Dutton and Jim Collins and organizations like Gallup. I use many of their principles in my coaching practice and know they work.

The Coach's Clipboard is meant to help you develop and implement your own leadership plan—and also to help you as you coach your own team. That's part of leadership, too, and you can draw on these pointers to help you do that.

My goal is to be inclusive and informative, to have a little fun and, most of all, to offer advice that is practical and effective.

The Coach's Clipboard

Have a dream

A dream is bigger than a goal. It's in the realm of things that you really don't know are even possible and that may seem virtually unattainable. Think of it as a BHAG—Big Hairy Audacious Goal—a term coined by authors Jim Collins and Jerry Porras.

My friends John and Jan Kosta grew up near New York City. As children, they loved the city but never imagined they could afford to live there. They raised four children in Michigan but continued to dream of living in Manhattan. Several years after they told me about their secret wish, my wife and I got a card from them. They were inviting us to come visit them in their new apartment on the 17th floor of a building overlooking Central Park. Several weeks later, over coffee in their new home, they told us the story of how several factors suddenly fell into place and their dream of moving to the Big Apple became reality.

My wife had the dream of visiting and writing about the Philippines—the birthplace of her grandfather, who had left in 1906 to join the U.S. Navy and never returned. Almost 100 years to the day after his departure, Pat returned as an author to investigate her family's story. Eventually, that led to her giving a presentation at the Smithsonian on the history of Filipinos in the U.S. Navy.

One set of clients told me of their dream to develop the world's best artificial heart. At the time, this Japanese start-up company consisted of a handful of international scientists. That was in 2000. Today, Terumo Heart Inc. is manufacturing the

DuraHeart, a rotary blood pump for long-term patient support, in Ann Arbor, Mich. The device is being used in Japan and Europe and undergoing clinical trials in the United States. In less than 10 years, the company has realized many of its goals, saved lives and grown from 20 workers to 150.

Einstein knew the value of dreams, too. His advice? "Dare to dream."

The Playbook

→   Write down your dreams. You do have them, but sometimes it takes writing them down to realize that they are in your mind.

→   Formulate a dream about your company with colleagues.

→   Formulate a dream about something wonderful to strive for with your family.

→   Have a dream about where your life is headed with your significant other.

→   Tell others about your dream. Who knows—they may be able to help you make it come true.

Your Personal Playbook

Date:

Goal:

Motivation (why you are doing this):

Game Plan (how you will accomplish this):

Teammates (who will help):

Finish Line (when you will achieve this)

The Coach's Clipboard

Commit to your dream

2

T here's a famous quotation—apparently taken from the 1951 book *The Scottish Himalayan Expedition* by William H. Murray—that cuts to the heart of this principle:

> Until one is committed, there is hesitancy, the chance to draw back, always ineffectiveness. Concerning all acts of initiative (and creation) there is one elementary truth, the ignorance of which kills countless ideas and splendid plans: that the moment one definitely commits oneself, then Providence moves too. All sorts of things occur to help one that would never otherwise have occurred. A whole stream of events issues from the decision, raising in one's favor all manner of unforeseen incidents and meetings and material assistance, which no man could have dreamed would have come his way. I have learned a deep respect for one of Goethe's couplets:
>
> > Whatever you can do or dream you can, begin it.
> >
> > Boldness has genius, power and magic in it.

I've seen this play out in the life of a man who started a company but didn't leave his existing job and didn't really put a whole lot into the new business beyond hiring a few employees.

He loved the idea of having the firm, but it was more of a vanity business. Then one day, it looked as if he wouldn't be able to make the payroll. That came as a huge shock. He didn't want to close the business, but he realized he was going to have to make a greater commitment if he wanted it to succeed. I'd been encouraging him to hire a CEO and so he finally did, giving up a piece of the company in the process. But his greater commitment and the moves he made as a result revived the company.

Sometimes it takes hitting bottom before people make a commitment, but it's much better if you don't wait that long. Those who never truly make a commitment never achieve their dreams.

The Playbook

→ Recognize the distinction between a to-do list and a dream. A dream is bigger. You have to feel some passion for it. It's the kind of thing that makes you nervous. You know it's not going to be easy. But no dream is going to come true by accident. You're going to have to dig deep and risk something.

→ Don't just go through the motions. A friend started a business, drew up the legal papers, had business cards and brochures printed—and couldn't understand why he had no clients. But he wasn't devoting full time to finding them. He hadn't risked a thing.

→ Develop a plan and implement it. You don't need the best plan to succeed, just a good one executed with precision.

→ When making decisions, ask yourself a question that one of my clients, banker Gary Haapala, likes to use: Am I running away from something or toward something? Toward is usually better.

Your Personal Playbook

Date:

Goal:

Motivation (why you are doing this):

Game Plan (how you will accomplish this):

Teammates (who will help):

Finish Line (when you will achieve this)

The Coach's Clipboard

Define your passion

I n his book *Good to Great*, Jim Collins famously compares great leaders to hedgehogs. Unlike the wily fox of the underlying fable, hedgehogs are determined, single-minded souls. They know who they are (and who they are not), and they stick to a path, pursuing one great idea. Their self-awareness is strong and clear. How do they get to that point? Collins says they do it by asking themselves three questions:

1. What am I passionate about?
2. What talents enable me to be the best in the world at what I do? (And what won't I be the best in the world at?)
3. Financially, how much is enough, and how can I make a living applying my passion and my unique talent?

My friend Mike Pape introduced me to *Good to Great*, and he is a great example of a hedgehog.

Mike knew what his passion was—finding a cure for heart disease, which had killed many members of his family—and what his talents were. So, he became a world-class scientist, part of the team that developed the cholesterol-fighting drug Lipitor. Mike wasn't driven to accumulate wealth, but he wanted to provide enough for his children and his church. So, in the late 1990s, he cofounded Esperion Therapeutics Inc., an Ann Arbor pharmaceutical company that was acquired by Pfizer Inc. in a billion-dollar-plus transaction in 2004. Today, Mike is still pursuing his great idea as the head of a venture capital fund that underwrites biotech research.

The Playbook

→ Notice what brings you the most joy in life. That's likely what your passion is.

→ Being "best in the world" is a tall order, but if you think about "your world" as opposed to "the world," it becomes easier. Think "best in your company," "best on your team," "best in your class." Now, that's a scale you can work with.

→ Identifying what you *aren't* best at, and probably never will be, is just as important. Too often we spend too much time striving to overcome our weaknesses instead of developing our strengths.

→ Develop yourself and your team. Every day ask yourself: Have I mentored someone or contributed in some way to the development of others?

→ Appeal to other people's highest ideals, hopes, dreams and passions. That's how great leaders inspire. "We cannot inspire passion in others without engaging in it ourselves," writes Richard Boyatzis, coauthor of *Primal Leadership: Learning to Lead with Emotional Intelligence*.

Your Personal Playbook

Date:

Goal:

Motivation (why you are doing this):

Game Plan (how you will accomplish this):

Teammates (who will help):

Finish Line (when you will achieve this)

The Coach's Clipboard

Honor other people's dreams

One of the most effective ways to honor others' dreams is to foster team spirit. Bring your team together and draw out each member—who they are as people, what they're about, what interests they have besides work, what their family histories are. Take the time to get to know them.

The objective is to get everyone to understand each other's goals and dreams beyond work and to get people to talk to each other. Team members draw closer. They learn to build each other up, not drag each other down.

One of my clients was preparing for an off-site outing of about 10 members of his staff. To break the ice, he thought about just asking each person to say something about themselves. But that can be tough for people who seize up when put on the spot. I suggested that he get each person to write down on a card something unusual about themselves, something that another person wouldn't guess, and then to put the cards in a hat and pass it around. Each person would pick a card and try to guess who wrote it.

Someone might reveal that they're a diehard Harley-Davidson rider or writing a romance novel in the garret at midnight. Or—in my case—that O.J. Simpson once recognized *me* on the street. (It was as I came off an appearance on the *Today Show* in the early 1990s and he was going into the studio after just watching the show.)

The point is: You may think you know someone, but you may not. It's upbeat and fun and takes the pressure off. And once you've broken the ice, get your team members to talk about their dreams. Someone may have a chronic illness and is looking for a way to reach out to others. Someone else may want to build a vacation home on a mountaintop in North Carolina or work with Habitat for Humanity in Africa. If you get people to reveal their secret longings, you honor them as more than worker bees and you never know what connections might be made as a result. Maybe someone else in the group can help them move a step closer to fulfilling their dream.

The Playbook

→ You can never communicate too much, so make the rounds regularly to check in with your team, your family and your friends. Find out what's on their minds.

→ Meetings are great, but a lot of important communication occurs informally. Look for ways to make that happen.

→ Honor your employees' dreams. Pass along information or just ask periodically how things are going. When employees feel respected and valued, it's that much easier for them to reach out with care and to really listen to clients and customers.

→ Treat everyone from the lowest-paid worker to the highest-paid exec with respect, and treat them the same.

→ Listen to your children. They have dreams too, but you may have to ask searching questions to draw them out.

Your Personal Playbook

Date:

Goal:

Motivation (why you are doing this):

Game Plan (how you will accomplish this):

Teammates (who will help):

Finish Line (when you will achieve this)

The Coach's Clipboard

Learn people's stories

O ral historian Alan Lomax once said, "The essence of America is not within the headline heroes ... but in the everyday folks who live and die unknown, yet leave their dreams as legacies."

Everyone has a story, and if you take the time as a leader to discover them, you will forge strong bonds. Ask simple questions—"Where'd you grow up?" "How many people are in your family?" Pay attention to little things.

When meeting a new client, I make it a point to look around the person's office. One time, I saw a Detroit Tigers pennant poster from the 1930s. I'm a Tigers fan, so I asked about it. That led to a discussion of how the man found the poster when his wife took him to an antiques show. And then I noticed a newspaper article about a boy with Down syndrome. So I asked whether it was the man's son, and he said yes. I told him I'd worked with Down cases and had done my dissertation on this. And so we spent half an hour talking about his son and his achievements. We had an instant bond.

David Meitz, who was a manager at Reuters at the time of the Sept. 11, 2001, terrorist attacks, lost colleagues in the collapse of the World Trade Center. Even though he supervised about 100 people, he was deeply troubled by the fact that he could not come up with a mental picture of one of his missing team members. Meitz, now chief technology officer for Investment Technology Group Inc., vowed that he wouldn't let it happen again and that he would always get to know the stories and the faces of those who report to him.

The Playbook

→ Ask people about their lives—and listen to their answers. "If you take the time to listen, you'll find wisdom, wonder and poetry in their lives," writes David Isay in *Listening Is an Act of Love*.

→ Ask family members about their day. Listen especially closely to your children when they respond. Their stories are never mundane to them.

→ Ask people about the family pictures they have on their desks.

→ People generally love recounting tales from the past. Get them to open up with simple questions about their families and where they once lived or went to school.

→ Look around. Notice what people are wearing or what's in their office. What you see is a jumping off point for a conversation.

→ Learn to ask the kinds of questions that get people talking about themselves.

→ Tell your own stories, including those of people who helped you get where you are today.

→ Keep in mind these words from Gabriel Garcia Marquez: "What matters most in life is not what happens to you, but what you remember and how you remember it."

Your Personal Playbook

Date:

Goal:

Motivation (why you are doing this):

Game Plan (how you will accomplish this):

Teammates (who will help):

Finish Line (when you will achieve this)

The Coach's Clipboard

Keep rewriting your story

S cott and his wife, Sue, made major changes in their lives to restore balance. They left careers and a busy life in Washington, D.C., to earn post-graduate degrees in Michigan. But they soon learned that nothing is set in stone. As time went on and life kept intervening, they had to keep recentering their lives, rewriting their script.

A start-up business replaced the demands of the university. A new home replaced student housing. Raising children replaced a more carefree life—and brought a host of new responsibilities and commitments.

"We quickly found the trap of too many priorities and so scaled back (painfully, as they were important to us) to the most important, our center of gravity," Scott says. Making adjustments to accommodate the unexpected is often the only choice, he says, and "accepting this fact opens the door to feeling successful and, ironically, balanced."

The Playbook

→ Are you putting as much into your home life as your work life? If not, make adjustments. Get home before the kids are in bed. Spend more time with them on weekends. Dedicate one weekend day just to them. Pick them up at school.

→ Family life is unpredictable. If you schedule yourself too fully, there is no real family time left. Allow for the unexpected.

→ Look around your community. Is it where you really want to live? Pick a community that accurately reflects your values.

→ Throughout your life, you'll have to make adjustments to sustain your health. Don't neglect to factor this into your schedule.

→ Your personal center of gravity is all about values. Discuss with the most important people in your life what you want to be your priorities going forward.

Your Personal Playbook

Date:

Goal:

Motivation (why you are doing this):

Game Plan (how you will accomplish this):

Teammates (who will help):

Finish Line (when you will achieve this)

The Coach's Clipboard

Accept your leadership role

When people assume leadership positions, it's as if they morph instantly in the eyes of those around them. It's what best-selling author Daniel Goleman defines as "primal leadership" in his books on this theme. Groups of people expect to be led, and they bestow that responsibility on the person labeled their leader. But the designation can be short-lived if the leader fails to step up.

This happened to me in a small way when I was asked to give a presentation to a group at a company. I began to address the group while sitting down. Then the woman who had invited me said, "Rob, aren't you going to stand up?" The expectation was that I would lead a more formal presentation, and I had to accept that responsibility.

These expectations extend to other trappings of leadership as well. One of my clients who'd been appointed a vice president of his company was still wearing his worn, old clothing to work. I told him that he wasn't going to get the respect of his team until he lived up to their expectations—and that included taking the wardrobe up a few notches.

If leaders fail to step up to the norms, someone will challenge their authority.

The Playbook

→ Get feedback. Ask people how they perceive you as a leader.

→ Take a look in the mirror. You are not the same person you were the day before you took on your new role, so look at what you see with new eyes. Be critical and assess what changes you need to make.

→ If you want to be a leader but feel as though you are "selling out," find out where the line is—the one you don't want to cross. Chances are you can change a few things and still be true to your values.

→ Don't dress down. If you don't know the etiquette, ask questions. Learn what is expected in a given situation.

→ Remember common-sense don'ts—don't be overly flirtatious, don't make coarse jokes.

→ Realize that you can't afford to live in a shell. As a leader, you're always "on," even when you don't want to be.

→ Avoid sarcasm. Others may easily misunderstand.

Your Personal Playbook

Date:

Goal:

Motivation (why you are doing this):

Game Plan (how you will accomplish this):

Teammates (who will help):

Finish Line (when you will achieve this)

The Coach's Clipboard

Develop daily practices and family rituals

8

Many leaders work at balancing their lives through what they call daily practices. These can be tiny habits or big ones. Usually they are sprinkled throughout the day as a way to stop and reconnect, if only for a moment.

Here's what Shlynn, who attended one of my workshops, told me she does every day:

- Affirmation.
- Meditation (at least 10 minutes).
- Begin the day with an attitude of gratitude.
- Practice breathing in positive energy and breathing out negative energy.
- Work smarter not harder.
- End the day by giving thanks.

My friend Peggy Began, who is a nurse at the Cleveland Clinic, developed a daily practice with a coworker where they challenge themselves to do three things: Learn something new, do something helpful and have fun. This helped Peggy become more positive and balanced.

As you can see, these practices need not be heavy or overbearing. They can be whatever you want them to be, as long as they ease your way through the day. And don't limit them to your hours at work. They're also a part of developing family traditions and rituals.

When our kids were little, Saturday was "candy day." Sweets were off limits during the week, but on Saturdays, we'd head to the confectionery store where we'd let the boys pick out something special. It became a family outing and lots of fun.

The Playbook

→ When you read or hear a useful idea, write it down in your own words; then translate it into actions that fit into your life.

→ Be mindful of the drama of everyday life and alert to its surprises.

→ In any encounter with another, search for what you can learn, enjoy and appreciate.

→ Spend some time every day practicing that which is most sacred to you.

→ Use your calendar to keep track of your daily rituals and any anecdotes or thoughts related to them.

→ Celebrate the arrival of each new season in some special way with family or friends.

→ Make a list of simple things you can do for yourself: breathe, stretch, wash your face, give yourself a massage, close your eyes for a few seconds.

→ Look for ways every day to do something spiritual, physical, intellectual and fun.

Your Personal Playbook

Date:

Goal:

Motivation (why you are doing this):

Game Plan (how you will accomplish this):

Teammates (who will help):

Finish Line (when you will achieve this)

The Coach's Clipboard

Think before you act

I n his book *The Path of Least Resistance*, business consultant Robert Fritz advises taking time before you act to ask yourself a key question: What result do I wish to create? Leaders often forget that their actions can have a bigger impact than they imagined or intended. Sometimes actions bring the desired positive outcome; other times, they trigger unanticipated negative consequences. Identifying and focusing on achieving positive results will greatly enhance your capacity to be an effective leader.

I'm a verbal guy and a lot of times I'll just say what's on my mind. But sometimes I fail to consider the impact this may have. I don't stop to ask myself what result I want to create—and I do mean "create." Communication is about creating. When you interact with people, you create an action or reaction. If you don't think about what you're saying ahead of time, you may trigger a reaction that you didn't intend.

If I want to bring up a delicate subject with my wife, I first need to stop and think: Why do I want to bring this up? Do I just want to get it off my chest and make it her problem or do I want some help with it? Is this a good time to broach it or should I wait and think it through a while longer?

Say you want to raise prices for your product or service. You must consider both the upside and downside of the move. You may simply want to generate more revenue, but have you considered the impact on customers who can't or don't want to pay the higher price? Are you prepared to lose them? How can you keep them or win them back?

Sometimes leaders are too bold and impulsive. They jump into something too quickly. This also happens in families. Maybe your daughter has busted curfew once too often, so you say, "That's it! You're not going out any more after 9 o'clock. I set the rules." But what if your daughter starts sneaking out? What if she's out after 9 and you don't know it? Is that the result you wanted? Is there a better solution?

The Playbook

→ Write down what you're trying to do. Ask yourself: If I'm successful at this, what will happen? Is this the result that I want?

→ As you make decisions, take the long view. Are your daily actions aligned with your long-term goals?

→ Carry this idea over to your family life. Don't make off-the-cuff remarks that may hurt your loved ones. Think before you speak.

→ If you're involved in community activities, evaluate whether this is a good use of your time by asking yourself whether the work is bringing the results you want.

→ Use this approach when you set up a personal program to improve your health. What do you want to work on and what outcomes do you wish to have? Set some parameters.

Your Personal Playbook

Date:

Goal:

Motivation (why you are doing this):

Game Plan (how you will accomplish this):

Teammates (who will help):

Finish Line (when you will achieve this)

The Coach's Clipboard

Inspire, don't intimidate

S ome leaders achieve great success by intimidating people. It may work for a while, but as with any dictatorship, it's not sustainable. You can't just look at results. You have to look below the surface.

Some of the companies I work with use culture surveys where employees write down anonymously how they feel about a leader or a department. These devices are pretty sensitive at detecting morale problems.

In one case, a highly successful executive was hired away by another company on the basis of his past performance. But in the new setting, people under him soon started quitting or getting sick and taking extended leaves. The culture survey pointed to his intimidating management style.

Research shows you can get a child to do anything by force and intimidation, but it's not conducive to healthy development. It's the same at work. You need an approach that inspires good work, not dictates it.

The Playbook

→ Review your mission statement. Check with your staff to see if it appeals to their highest ideals, hopes and dreams. If it doesn't, have them help rewrite the statement to be more inspiring.

→ To the best of your ability, give your staff the support and resources it needs.

→ Empower people to adjust to circumstances as they arise and not wait for orders from above.

→ Lead by enabling those under you to focus on what they do best. Let them shine.

→ Remember that constant criticism can kill an organization.

→ Don't forget that your family's hopes and dreams need encouragement, too. Always listen intently and never try to diminish their aspirations.

→ Give more rewards (and fewer punishments) to your children.

→ Support your friends when they are down; acknowledge their successes when they're up.

Your Personal Playbook

Date:

Goal:

Motivation (why you are doing this):

Game Plan (how you will accomplish this):

Teammates (who will help):

Finish Line (when you will achieve this)

The Coach's Clipboard

Fill those buckets

11

Authors Tom Rath and Donald O. Clifton used research by the Gallup Organization to craft the bestseller *How Full Is Your Bucket?*

Their basic theory is that we start out every day with a bucket that is emptied or filled by what others say and do to us. We each also have a dipper. We can use it to fill other people's buckets by delivering positive messages or we can dip from others' buckets by delivering negative messages. When we fill others' buckets, we replenish our own. And when we take from others' buckets, we deplete our own.

The process is contagious. If you fill others' buckets with positive messages, they will carry it forward. So, if you work for me and I build you up, you're more likely to build up the people you come in contact with. If I drain your bucket, you're more likely to dump on others.

Marvin rose through the ranks to lead a unit of his company. He was extremely popular in part because he was so positive with people. He saw his ability to encourage people as a major focus of his life. He made it his mission. He wasn't afraid to confront people when necessary, but he tried to be more positive than negative.

When there was an opening to move higher in the organization, Marvin was one of many candidates considered. In the end, he got the job in part because of the trail of good feelings he had left behind him. Don't misunderstand—Marvin wasn't a flatterer. His weren't empty gestures. He sincerely tried to make a difference, and in the end, he benefited as much as anyone.

The Playbook

→ People remember and respect those who make them feel special. If you can't show appreciation, people won't stick around. You really have only three choices when you respond to others: praise, ignore or criticize.

→ Keep track of the abundances of your day—the times when someone has been nice to you or when you've done someone a favor, when a meeting has gone particularly well or when you've offered someone praise or encouragement. Jot them down on your computer or in a notepad in your purse or wallet.

→ Be genuine about your praise. Don't manufacture it for the sake of appearances.

→ Keep in mind research by psychologist John Gottman that shows healthy relationships have a ratio of five positive interactions for every negative one. So if you're handing out more corrections than pats on the back, people are going to start feeling bad about themselves. When you come in the room, they're going to want to duck, whether it's your employees or your kids.

→ Be specific about what you praise. Highlight a report the person submitted or a comment they made in a meeting.

→ Turn a negative into a positive. If you notice someone seems out of sorts or is struggling, ask what's wrong. Find out what kind of help they need or whether they have the resources to get the job done.

→ Keep track of your own daily achievements, however small.

→ Remember: Nine out of 10 people say they're more productive when they're around positive people.

→ Fill another's bucket and you automatically fill your own.

→ Smile. Nothing gives as much happiness as the gift of awareness.

Your Personal Playbook

Date:

Goal:

Motivation (why you are doing this):

Game Plan (how you will accomplish this):

Teammates (who will help):

Finish Line (when you will achieve this)

The Coach's Clipboard

Recognize your blind spots

Research shows that often it's not what we see but what we fail to see that causes us to self-destruct. So it's really important to become aware of our blind spots.

- Are you a perfectionist who can never admit your failings?
- Do you teeter constantly on the brink of burnout because you overdo everything?
- Are you so power-hungry that you'd fire your mom to win points with the boss?
- Do you micromanage people (even your family) to the point where they'd seriously like to do you bodily harm?

One of my clients had an upsetting event at work that led him to believe certain people disliked him. In our coaching work, we zeroed in on the problem: Ty was hung up on the idea that he should be loved by everybody for everything he did—no exceptions. He couldn't seem to get past this blind spot until we talked it through. Finally, he realized that he had to let it go and accept the fact that not everyone was going to like him.

The Playbook

→ Poll people who have known you for a long time and ask them to help you identify your blind spots.

→ Be aware of the self-defeating patterns that can be triggered by blind spots. Teach yourself to let go.

→ Once you are aware of your blind spots, keep them in mind as you make decisions and interact with others. Ask: Is there any aspect of this where I am giving in to a blind spot?

→ Recognize that you will never please everyone all of the time. Don't spend hours worrying about what never will be.

→ Give yourself permission to be imperfect.

Your Personal Playbook

Date:

Goal:

Motivation (why you are doing this):

Game Plan (how you will accomplish this):

Teammates (who will help):

Finish Line (when you will achieve this)

The Coach's Clipboard

Know your emotional IQ

M any leaders tend to be competitive, hard-driving people. They have high intellectual IQs, but sometimes their emotional IQs lag behind. I coached one manager who had been one of the most successful salespeople at a financial services company. He'd been promoted to manager and was poised to move up to the next level. But as I worked with him, I quickly saw that he lacked the ability to connect well with others.

One of the dimensions of emotional intelligence is whether you are aware of your own feelings. This man always put on a happy face. If you asked him how he was doing, he'd always say, "Perfect!" He wasn't attuned to the subtleties of his own emotional life because he'd taught himself to simply put on a positive front.

He also wasn't able to read the emotions of others well. He had no sense of the impact his words might have. He'd do things like overdo teasing to the point where it became offensive.

He also was weak on his ability to manage his emotions. He could fly off the handle in an instant and would make no attempt to rein himself in. In fact, he thought yelling at people was the way to motivate them. Instead, he just made everyone afraid of him.

He also fell down on his ability to manage the emotions of the group, which is one of the most difficult things to do. A lot of the work of leaders involves managing a team or a meeting.

It's almost like being an orchestra conductor—sensing how the group is feeling, knowing when to call on someone, recognizing who hasn't been participating. Drawing people out is a delicate art. My client could manage these situations at times, but then he'd have a major blowup and publicly humiliate someone.

The Playbook

→ Keep a mood log. Several times a day, write down how you are feeling. Look back at the end of the week and assess how tuned in you were to your own emotions.

→ Avoid shaming others. It can be highly destructive.

→ At work or at home, make a point of empathizing with others. Put yourself in that person's shoes. Think about what it would feel like to be that person.

→ If you're having a dispute, look at it from the other person's viewpoint. Try writing out a narrative of the disagreement from the other standpoint.

→ Avoid psychologist John Gottman's *Four Horsemen of the Apocalypse*: criticism, defensiveness, contempt and stonewalling. Gottman found that these four attitudes, especially in combination, are predictors of which marriages will fail. They're equally bad in the work setting.

Your Personal Playbook

Date:

Goal:

Motivation (why you are doing this):

Game Plan (how you will accomplish this):

Teammates (who will help):

Finish Line (when you will achieve this)

The Coach's Clipboard

Figure out where your role begins— and ends

I once was tapped for help because the CEO of a company—a very talented entrepreneur—was so heavily micromanaging his staff that they were ready to revolt. He thought he could do anything better than anyone else. As a result, he wasn't letting anyone else do their job.

I asked the CEO to complete a simple exercise in which he listed the duties his job description covered and those it didn't cover. I asked his executive team to do the same thing because I wanted to see where there was agreement.

By the time the CEO had finished, his list had 25 items on it—instead of the six or eight it should have had. I could see a light bulb go on in his head.

I worked with him for six weeks, helping him find ways to feel comfortable letting go while clarifying his own vital role in the company. We set up a daily schedule using pie charts to help him focus on four or five major tasks.

Letting go wasn't easy for him and he sometimes resisted strenuously, but he eventually got the hang of it. His leadership team is still together.

The Playbook

→ Do the "my job, not my job" exercise with each of your direct reports.

→ Do the "my job, not my job" exercise with family members.

→ Be accountable. Whatever your job is, or whatever the other person's job is, say what you will do and do what you say.

→ Figure out what you love doing and find or create a job where you can do it most of the time.

→ Focus on what you *can* do, tasks you can achieve and situations you can influence. Don't dwell on things you *can't* do.

Your Personal Playbook

Date:

Goal:

Motivation (why you are doing this):

Game Plan (how you will accomplish this):

Teammates (who will help):

Finish Line (when you will achieve this)

The Coach's Clipboard

Look out the window and in the mirror

I n *Good to Great*, Jim Collins describes the highest level of leadership, what he calls Level 5. What characterizes these folks, Collins says, is the ability to blend "extreme personal humility with intense professional will." Collins uses the concept of the window and mirror to explain how these leaders are able to use those qualities to focus and succeed.

The rationale behind the concept is that leaders must look out the window when it comes to giving credit for successes—that is, look outside themselves, to their teams, when things go well. And when things don't go well, leaders must look first in the mirror to assign responsibility.

I have used this technique many times in coaching, because it is so illuminating and the image so easy to grasp. Clients have reported dramatic changes when they start to incorporate this into their thinking. They set their egos aside and give credit where it is due. They retrain their minds so they don't automatically blame others for failures or glitches.

Nelson Mandela put it another way: "It is better to lead from behind and to put others in front, especially when you celebrate victory when nice things occur. You take the front line when there is danger. Then people will appreciate your leadership."

The Playbook

→ Consistently give credit for successes to your team.

→ After a failure, scrutinize your own actions first.

→ Give your family credit for your—and their—successes.

→ Look for ways to help your family and friends through their failures.

→ Just keep telling yourself it's not all about you.

→ Coach others on the window-mirror test. Ask them to hold you to this standard.

Your Personal Playbook

Date:

Goal:

Motivation (why you are doing this):

Game Plan (how you will accomplish this):

Teammates (who will help):

Finish Line (when you will achieve this)

The Coach's Clipboard

Foster a learning environment

M any of my coaching clients make it a practice to select a book every quarter or so for their leadership teams to read and discuss. Sometimes I've helped the process by working with the team to assign projects, exercises, discussions and presentations based on a particular book. This helps focus everyone's energies on understanding and applying the relevant messages.

Through the Internet, leaders today find it easy to pass along articles and other information that they find helpful and pertinent. This creates a communication chain in which communities of people share and expand their pool of knowledge.

When an organization becomes what is called a "learning organization," it dedicates itself to a continual process of learning new things, learning from mistakes and learning from objective data. I use this concept extensively with companies. It's an ongoing process of sharing and learning, and feedback is crucial. It amounts to a continual practice of reading, learning, evaluating and altering what you do according to the feedback you get.

Google is a great example of a company that is constantly churning the waters, trying new things, launching new products, setting up creative work environments, hiring top people and so on. When companies or governments stop the learning process, alarm bells should go off, because that is when rigidity sets in.

Failing to change and adapt in today's fast-paced world can be fatal.

The Playbook

- → Set up a business-related book discussion group. (Some worthwhile titles are listed in the back of this book.)

- → Turn your company into a learning organization: a place where people continually learn from each other, continually change as the environment changes and where there is dedication to educating the workforce and the customers.

- → Design your workspace so that it stimulates innovation and collaboration.

- → Turn your family into a learning organization. Read and talk about books and articles that are age-appropriate. Not only is this fun, but it teaches kids how to put on their thinking caps, form opinions and express themselves.

- → Create a learning organization in your neighborhood or community. Set up a mechanism for working on common issues and problems.

- → Always have a good, non-work-related book to read.

Your Personal Playbook

Date:

Goal:

Motivation (why you are doing this):

Game Plan (how you will accomplish this):

Teammates (who will help):

Finish Line (when you will achieve this)

The Coach's Clipboard

Know your limits

I f you know your limits—your challenges as well as your strengths—you'll spend far less time trying to be someone you aren't and doing things you aren't likely to succeed at. We have a tendency to overvalue the things we're not particularly good at and undervalue what comes naturally.

One man became president and CEO of his company, but he wasn't entirely comfortable with some of the hats he had to wear. He wasn't great at networking, though he was excellent with numbers and computers. So when the company needed help in that area, he was asked to consider stepping aside as CEO to become the chief technical officer. It might have been perceived as a demotion, but he saw the wisdom in the move. He made the shift and excelled in the new job. He felt much more valuable, he loved the work—and it was still a prestigious and important job.

People appreciate you for what you do, not your title.

The Playbook

→ Look back at your past failures and analyze what the components were. Where did you exceed your limits?

→ Hire people (or delegate to people) who are good at what you're not good at.

→ Decide how much time you can devote to work each week before feeling burned out.

→ Make a similar commitment to the hours you will spend with your family. Don't short-change them in favor of your job.

→ Volunteering can be wonderful, but it can drain your time and energy. Don't take on positions of leadership that cause you to exceed your limits.

→ Recognize that you can never be all things to all people all of the time, but if you budget your energy wisely, you can more often provide the right thing for the right person at the right time.

→ Know your financial limits. Spend beyond your means now and you commit yourself to work later.

→ Devise a plan for improving your health that is built realistically around your limits.

Your Personal Playbook

Date:

Goal:

Motivation (why you are doing this):

Game Plan (how you will accomplish this):

Teammates (who will help):

Finish Line (when you will achieve this)

The Coach's Clipboard

Control your temper

18

Marlin Fitzwater, who was a press secretary to Presidents Ronald Reagan and George H.W. Bush, once was interviewed on *Fresh Air* on National Public Radio, and he spoke about what great bosses both men were and, remarkably, how neither had ever lost his temper with Fitzwater.

Rarely does anyone relish a leader who can't control his temper. It's simply never appropriate or effective to get so exercised about something that you can't contain yourself. Angry explosions just scare people, and when they're scared, they're not productive. If you live in fear of the boss' wrath, you're working from a negative—"Let's not screw up or we're in for it"—instead of from a positive—"Let's do the best job we can and get the best results."

People sometimes think it's good to get things off their chest and that doing so in anger will improve the situation. But in my view, anger makes matters worse almost every time.

The Playbook

→ Don't expect to earn respect by losing your temper. Some great leaders who were known for outbursts—coaches Billy Martin, Bobby Knight and Woody Hayes come to mind—might have been even more successful had they exhibited control.

→ Consider getting professional help if you easily fly off the handle when criticized, feel like hitting someone when you're frustrated, think of yourself as hotheaded or say nasty things when you're annoyed.

→ Remember the Golden Rule. Do you like it when angry people come at you?

→ Keep track of the times when you manage to control your temper. It will give you insight into what triggers these situations and how you can gain the upper hand.

→ Ask calm folks how they manage to control their anger. Everyone feels anger. Only some act on it.

→ Drop and do pushups when you think you're about to blow your top.

Your Personal Playbook

Date:

Goal:

Motivation (why you are doing this):

Game Plan (how you will accomplish this):

Teammates (who will help):

Finish Line (when you will achieve this)

The Coach's Clipboard

Practice self-reflection

Meditation produces beneficial effects for the heart, brain and metabolic system, according to research done at Harvard Medical School and elsewhere. Anecdotal evidence also abounds about the positive effects of taking 10 or 15 minutes a day to slow the breathing and rest the body.

But meditation is only one of the ways to practice self-reflection. You may prefer to do it in connection with your faith. You may want to keep a journal. Or you may prefer talking with someone on a regular basis—your significant other, a friend or even another couple. Sometimes it's easier to be open and reflective with those who aren't part of your immediate family.

My wife and I see our longtime friends, Barry and Eileen, a few times a year, and we've developed a ritual as part of our get-togethers. We generally have dinner, and then everyone takes a turn, talking about what has happened in the intervening time and whatever else is on the person's mind. It is self-reflection, practiced within a group.

This has been very helpful over the years as we go through life's ups and downs. It's not all serious talk, either. We laugh a lot as well. Barry and Eileen have become part of our extended family.

The Playbook

→ Set aside time for reflection.

→ Find an activity—meditation, yoga, writing, prayer, conversation—that allows you to express your inner life.

→ Keep a journal.

→ Find an aid, perhaps a book or an online site, to help you and give you encouragement.

→ Turn to a 12-step program if you need help with an addiction.

→ Take advantage of faith-based spiritual retreats and study groups.

→ Talk to a therapist if you need special help.

→ Take a class to learn ways to stimulate self-reflection.

→ Use your drive time for reflection.

Your Personal Playbook

Date:

Goal:

Motivation (why you are doing this):

Game Plan (how you will accomplish this):

Teammates (who will help):

Finish Line (when you will achieve this)

The Coach's Clipboard

Ask when enough is enough

S ome people compulsively compare themselves to others; they never think about what is enough in terms of their own satisfaction. They figure they need to strive for more, more, more—instead of recognizing that they already may have more than 90% of the people on the planet. They never stop to ask themselves: Is this how I want my life to be?

It's not just about money. It can be about achievement or prestige. It can even be about toys. I've got a perfectly good phone. It does everything I need it to do. But when the iPhone came out, people said, "Oh, you should have an iPhone, because it does this and this and this." I needed to stop and think: Do I really need it? Do I need to spend $400 on a new toy? Is it going to take me months to figure out how to use it? And how long before the next new toy comes along? (I decided to pass on the iPhone for the moment.)

I usually use junky pens because I lose them right and left. But a friend once gave me an expensive pen because he thought it would better fit my station in life. I was terrified I would lose the pen, and sure enough, it vanished soon after he gave it to me. But I couldn't tell him that, so I went out and bought a replacement. The status symbol had become a kind of burden.

The Playbook

→ Get in the habit of comparing yourself downward as well as upward. Think about how much more you have than others.

→ Travel to poorer parts of the world. It will help you appreciate what you have. Don't just go to the resort in Jamaica; drive around and see how ordinary people live.

→ Don't just give money to a charitable cause—get close to the people it serves. Work at the shelter or the food bank; don't just send a check. Bring your kids along.

→ Remember where you came from. Always appreciate how far you've come—and how far you have to go.

Your Personal Playbook

Date:

Goal:

Motivation (why you are doing this):

Game Plan (how you will accomplish this):

Teammates (who will help):

Finish Line (when you will achieve this)

The Coach's Clipboard

Own your idiosyncrasies

I'm a messy person by nature. Maybe it's the way my brain is wired. But I have to recognize that, while I can live with my messiness, others can't. If I leave my soggy towels in a heap on the bathroom floor, I'm not being respectful of others.

It's important to be aware of the impact we have on others. Beyond that, it's important to take responsibility for accommodating the styles and tastes of others. This is true up and down the ladder. If you're in charge, you can't just impose your will. Leaders sometimes think they can dictate the terms of everything. That doesn't work very well. At any level, it's important to cultivate an awareness of the expectations of others and how you should respond and adjust.

Karen likes to get things done just in time, not a minute too soon, and she makes no apologies for doing so. "That's how I am!" she says of her last-minute work. But her habits give her supervisor, Joan, a lot of anxiety and don't afford Joan the opportunity to check Karen's work to help her improve. So it's really not OK for Karen to just toss off the issue in a like-it-or-lump-it way. Her boss is a by-the-book person, and Karen should be respectful of and responsive to those expectations.

The Playbook

→ Accept the fact that you have idiosyncrasies. We all do.

→ Recognize that sometimes you can let your idiosyncrasies run rampant and sometimes you can't.

→ Make the adjustments you need to accommodate others' styles and tastes.

→ Focus on what you know needs to be done to improve yourself—and do it.

→ If you're not sure about your habits and the effect they have on others, ask people who really know you.

Your Personal Playbook

Date:

Goal:

Motivation (why you are doing this):

Game Plan (how you will accomplish this):

Teammates (who will help):

Finish Line (when you will achieve this)

The Coach's Clipboard

Follow the New Golden Rule

T he Old Golden Rule was: Do unto others as you would have them do unto you. It's still a good one, but the Gallup Organization added a New Golden Rule: Do unto others as *they* would have you do unto *them*.

Here's an example: You decide that because you love to get money as a gift, you're going to give everybody on your staff money to reward their achievements and they'll find that just as motivating as you do. The problem is that there is no single motivator that applies to everyone. Money is a great motivator for some people, but not for everyone.

In general, people are motivated by three things: achievement (winning at competition), affiliation (being part of a team) or power (status, influence). Usually two of these motivators are strong in a person and the third isn't. So if you use a reward system built on just one thing, you're not likely to catch everybody.

Lori is a sales manager who was struggling to find a way to motivate her staff. She had set up a monetary reward system tied to sales volume, but it didn't seem to spur anyone on. I asked her about her staff, and it turned out that they all really loved being part of a team—and so did Lori. So I suggested she use an "affiliation" reward system and have her three staffers work together on the sales goals and split the monetary reward. They achieved their team goal in the first month.

When looking for ways to motivate your team, find out what the chief motivators are for the team. Don't just pick what you like the best. Let the team tell you.

The Playbook

→ Talk about the three motivators with your team. Ask them which ones are their prime motivators.

→ Ask each team member to describe what they think motivates each other member of the team.

→ At home, be sensitive to what motivates each family member. One person may respond very well to affection, but someone else may react much more positively when you give them a hand with a task.

→ When you make a mistake in the way you treat others, don't use the "yes, but" apology: "Yes, I was wrong, but you were also at fault." Use the "yes, and yes" approach: "Yes, I was wrong. And yes, I will make changes not to do it again." It's even OK to apologize in more than one way.

→ When it comes to power, share it with your spouse. When that doesn't happen, John Gottman's research shows, there's an 81% chance the marriage will fail.

Your Personal Playbook

Date:

Goal:

Motivation (why you are doing this):

Game Plan (how you will accomplish this):

Teammates (who will help):

Finish Line (when you will achieve this)

The Coach's Clipboard

Don't take people for granted

To often we come to expect that people will do their jobs because they are being paid for it and don't need special recognition.

Mira supervised people in the loan-processing area of an auto dealership. Her staff handled the documents generated by the sales staff, which depended on fast, reliable service to close the deals.

Mira recognized that her job was to remind the sales staff to acknowledge the hard work the loan processors were doing. So one day, the salespeople took the processors out for a thank-you lunch. Not only was the food great, but the back room staff appreciated the acknowledgement of their hard work by the people up front.

The Playbook

→ Acknowledge a job well done—at least verbally. A monetary reward (or tip, if you are a customer) may or may not be appropriate, but a "Thank you" and smile always are appreciated.

→ Think of small gifts and signs of appreciation you can give to those who provide you with a service. Don't wait until the holidays.

→ Learn the names of those who provide your services. They know yours—do you know theirs?

→ Be specific in your praise, for example: "Thanks for staying late to process that paperwork. It made all the difference in getting the job done."

Your Personal Playbook

Date:

Goal:

Motivation (why you are doing this):

Game Plan (how you will accomplish this):

Teammates (who will help):

Finish Line (when you will achieve this)

The Coach's Clipboard

If you're stuck, get unstuck

L iving in today's world requires almost a constant process of change. If you can't adapt, you stagnate. It's what Robert E. Quinn calls "slow death" in his book *Deep Change: Discovering the Leader Within.* He says we often face a choice: Accept the status quo—"slow death"—or embark on a deep change, which he likens to "walking naked into a land of uncertainty."

Are you caught in such a dilemma?

I grappled with these issues a number of years ago when I contemplated leaving my work as a clinical psychologist and becoming an executive leadership coach. I was afraid to make the break because it would throw my income into uncertainty. But then I heard Quinn give a speech in which he talked about building the bridge as you walk on it (also the title of another of his books). I realized that if I didn't give up my clinical practice, I would never make the change. Quinn inspired me to step out onto that invisible bridge. I did, and I had a few scary months, but everything worked out in the end.

The Playbook

→ If you find that you aren't cut out for a certain task or job, don't be afraid to ask to be reassigned. You may end up in a better place.

→ Set up a strategic plan for making a big change. Write it down. Share it with knowledgeable people and get their input. Revise, rework and implement.

→ Be aware of times when you are avoiding something because it isn't in your comfort zone. This could apply to a wide range of situations, including your family life. Commit yourself to making the needed change.

→ Keep in mind Quinn's advice that when we make deep changes, we have to trust that we will find the correct path, even if we don't have all the answers when we set out.

→ When it comes to health issues, don't throw up excuses. If you know you must make a big change or face the possibility of illness, just do it.

Your Personal Playbook

Date:

Goal:

Motivation (why you are doing this):

Game Plan (how you will accomplish this):

Teammates (who will help):

Finish Line (when you will achieve this)

The Coach's Clipboard

Feel the fear and do it anyway

W hat distinguishes really good leaders and entrepreneurs is that they feel fear, but they act anyway. Some of us have the misconception that people who are in those roles are fearless. What we don't realize is that these folks have trained themselves to recognize that fear is not a red light but a yellow caution light. You can give yourself permission to proceed once you've assessed the situation.

Zingerman's Deli cofounder Ari Weinzweig once told me that he feels fear every day—that a customer or client will be upset, that some new endeavor won't pan out—but he has trained himself to accept the feeling, not as a danger signal but as a sign of opportunity.

Randy Pausch, the Carnegie Mellon University computer science professor who died after battling pancreatic cancer, said there are barriers in life for good reason—to stop those who aren't meant to get past them. The rest will zoom on by.

In my view, there isn't much that's worth doing unless it challenges us and ignites that spark of fear.

The Playbook

→ Write down what you are afraid of and ask yourself: What's the worst that can happen if I do this?

→ Then ask yourself: If the worst did happen, could I handle it?

→ Be aware that some of the best leaders in the world feel the fear, just like you. Use fear as a positive motivator, not something that crushes your spirit.

→ Talk about your fears with others. You'll find that you're in a lot of good company.

→ Take to heart Marianne Williamson's words from *A Return to Love*: "Our deepest fear is not that we are inadequate. Our deepest fear is that we are powerful beyond measure. It is our light, not our darkness, that most frightens us. We ask ourselves, who am I to be brilliant, gorgeous, talented, fabulous? Actually, who are you not to be? … As we are liberated from our own fear, our presence automatically liberates others."

Your Personal Playbook

Date:

Goal:

Motivation (why you are doing this):

Game Plan (how you will accomplish this):

Teammates (who will help):

Finish Line (when you will achieve this)

The Coach's Clipboard

Don't make it all about you

A few days after the Sept. 11, 2001, terrorist attacks, I sat with Phil Lynch and the family of a member of his staff who was missing in the collapse of the World Trade Center. The young man had been attending a conference at the Windows on the World restaurant atop one of the towers when the planes struck. Phil had been appointed CEO of Reuters in the Americas only a few days before.

I marveled at the way Phil handled himself. He was compassionate, offering any help the family needed.

After that particularly difficult meeting with the family, I asked Phil how he had found the strength to manage the situation. He gave a very simple answer: "Rob, I just kept telling myself, 'It's not about me.' I knew my duty was to offer as much support to this grieving family as I could. Whenever I felt inadequate or unsure, I was able to steady myself by remembering that it's not about me—be there for them."

Phil's advice is something that anyone can draw on nearly every day, no matter what the setting or circumstance.

The Playbook

- → As a leader, remember that you have a sacred trust. It has to do with the people you lead, not you.

- → When in doubt, ask for guidance. You can do this through prayer, meditation, reflection and conversation.

- → Know your purpose. As best as you can, try to figure out why you are here at this moment and in this place.

- → Remember: We all look at situations first from the perspective that we are at the center of the universe. It takes effort to change this point of view.

- → Tell the people who help you regularly how much you appreciate them.

- → Honor your mentors.

Your Personal Playbook

Date:

Goal:

Motivation (why you are doing this):

Game Plan (how you will accomplish this):

Teammates (who will help):

Finish Line (when you will achieve this)

The Coach's Clipboard

Be like Warren

W hy did Warren Buffett sink billions into Goldman Sachs as other investment banking houses were failing left and right in the fall of 2008? Sure, Buffett stood to make a buck. (Probably lots of them.) But as he said in a statement announcing his action, he believed strongly in Goldman Sachs' "track record of outperformance."

Buffett has a track record, too—of investing in things that he believes in and letting market forces take care of the rest. He looks for opportunity even in an economic meltdown. There are lessons there for all of us.

The Playbook

→ Look for opportunities. According to USA Today, 16 of the 30 stocks that comprise the Dow Jones industrials were started during recessions, including AT&T (1875), General Electric (1878), Exxon (1882), 3M (1902), IBM (1911), Disney (1923), Hewlett-Packard (1938) and Microsoft (1975).

→ Invest in businesses where you do business. If you get a Dairy Queen three times a week (as I do), shouldn't you buy their stock?

→ Think globally, invest locally. Studies have shown that a greater percentage of the dollars spent at locally owned businesses stay in the community.

→ Bank locally. Local banks invest in your own community.

→ Buy locally grown or raised food. Help keep your money in the community.

Your Personal Playbook

Date:

Goal:

Motivation (why you are doing this):

Game Plan (how you will accomplish this):

Teammates (who will help):

Finish Line (when you will achieve this)

The Coach's Clipboard

Cultivate friendships

Despite my professional training, I've had difficulty expressing myself to friends. I tend to hide behind my therapist's mask. So, when an old friend, Nick, once chewed me out for being so silent while he had no problem talking about himself, I had to agree—and I thanked him for his honesty. He got me to work on this issue.

Men often have a terrible time cultivating friendships, but reconnecting with old friends and making and maintaining new ones is essential to our growth and development. Friends are vital to health and happiness; they can even help reduce stress.

Studies have shown that people who have intimate relationships are more likely to survive heart attacks and less likely to develop cancer and serious infections. There also is a strong correlation between a lack of social relationships and high blood pressure, smoking and obesity.

Without close friends, we battle loneliness and feel disconnected from the past. We often pine for the sense of connectedness we had as kids. Lots of things get in the way of maintaining friendships, including the competitive nature of our society, which promotes mistrust of others. But we should try diligently to resist these pressures.

The Playbook

→ Come to terms with your relationship with your parents, because these ties are the prototypes for your relationships with peers.

→ Reconnect with old friends and set up social gatherings with them.

→ Go to reunions.

→ Look for ways to open up to current friends: Plan a trip or outing. Talk about something you usually might not be inclined to bring up.

→ Identify the obstacles that tend to get in the way of your friendships: fear of rejection, unresolved conflicts, insufficient time, competitiveness, past failures.

→ Recognize that friendships aren't just about "being liked"; they're also about taking care of yourself by feeling connected to others.

→ Call at least one friend a week.

→ Do something—join a group, take a class, learn a new hobby or become a volunteer—that will put you in contact with others.

→ Don't create a situation where all of your friendships are tied to work or groups you belong to.

→ Be open and honest about yourself.

→ Make couple friendships and set up times to spend with couples you and your mate both like.

Your Personal Playbook

Date:

Goal:

Motivation (why you are doing this):

Game Plan (how you will accomplish this):

Teammates (who will help):

Finish Line (when you will achieve this)

The Coach's Clipboard

Mix and match personalities

P sychologists recognize four basic personality types:

- **Competitive:** Everything's a contest, and these folks like to win.
- **Collaborative:** These are the peacemakers; everything's an opportunity to build relationships.
- **Creative:** These are the innovators; everything's an opportunity to create.
- **Consistent:** These like order and routine; every situation is an opportunity to plan and improve order.

One type isn't better than another, just different. Most of us are a combination of two of these types and we may share some characteristics of a third.

So, for example, if you want to hold a retreat to generate a lot of new thinking and you put someone who is highly detail-oriented in charge, you may not get the result you want. The format won't be freewheeling enough to open the creative floodgates. Put that person on a financial report or a project where you need precision, but put a creative type in charge of the retreat.

The Playbook

→ Know the personality types on your team and strive for diversity.

→ Communities and neighborhoods have personalities, too. Live where you feel most comfortable or stimulated.

→ How you take care of your health can be keyed to your personality. Set up a routine that fits your type. Collaborators definitely need to join a team sport. Competitors need tough opponents. Consistent people need to keep a schedule—same time, same place. And you creative types—the world is your playground.

→ Opposites usually clash; competitive types clash with collaborative types; creative types with consistent types.

→ Hire managers for their collaborative skills. You can teach technical skills, but you can't teach compassion for the customer or fellow employees.

→ All of these personality types are needed for any endeavor to succeed.

Your Personal Playbook

Date:

Goal:

Motivation (why you are doing this):

Game Plan (how you will accomplish this):

Teammates (who will help):

Finish Line (when you will achieve this)

The Coach's Clipboard

Think positive

30

C ompassion, optimism, gratitude and forgiveness—those aren't words usually associated with the workplace. But research indicates companies that foster such attitudes are the newly successful ones. Google seems to be doing a pretty good job of it, for example.

Robert Quinn and his book *Deep Change* influenced the establishment of core values and a positive corporate culture. Kim Cameron, a professor of business and higher education at the University of Michigan, also has written extensively about organizational practices, including in his latest book, *Positive Leadership: Strategies for Extraordinary Performance*. His theory, supported by research, is that outcomes are better when work environments are supportive and upbeat.

Four years after selling Esperion Therapeutics, the highly successful Ann Arbor biotech company he cofounded, to Pfizer Inc. for $1.3 billion, scientist and researcher Roger Newton got Esperion's intellectual property back from Pfizer and raised $22.75 million in venture capital to restart the company in May 2008. (Newton had helped develop the best-selling cholesterol-fighting drug Lipitor and became Pfizer's senior vice president for global research and development after the sale of Esperion to the drug maker. But he was out of a job in 2007 when Pfizer underwent a global restructuring and decided to close Esperion along with its other Ann Arbor, Mich., facilities.)

Newton was a big fan of the theories of Quinn and Cameron. Quinn had helped Newton establish a positive corporate culture at Esperion built on key core values—individual dignity, vibrant teamwork and excellence in science—and Newton revived those principles after relaunching the company.

Keep in mind that embracing optimism and positive attitudes does not mean you should shield yourself from cold, hard realities. For too long, totally positive thinking kept leaders in the top echelons in this country from facing the truth that their financial practices were heading for deep trouble.

The Playbook

→ Talk to your team about ways to foster a positive environment. Make it a team project.

→ Discuss with your family the things that promote good feelings and plan activities around them.

→ Positive emotions promote good health, so by maximizing those things, you are making yourself healthier.

→ If someone constantly brings toxic emotions to the workplace, move that person out. One toxic person can poison the well.

→ The leader's mood is contagious. Choose a positive mood every day, but don't lose sight of reality.

Your Personal Playbook

Date:

Goal:

Motivation (why you are doing this):

Game Plan (how you will accomplish this):

Teammates (who will help):

Finish Line (when you will achieve this)

The Coach's Clipboard

Communicate in a crisis

31

Despite the obvious benefits of positive thinking, author Barbara Ehrenreich warned against its dangers in an op-ed piece she wrote for the New York Times: "No one was psychologically prepared for hard times when they hit, because, according to the tenets of positive thinking, even to think of trouble is to bring it on."

She advocated realism as the alternative—"seeing the risks, having the courage to bear bad news and being prepared for famine as well as plenty. We ought to give it a try."

One way to do that is to have a plan for hard times and to remember that the most important component is communication. I've seen this play out many times, but one of the most dramatic was in the aftermath of the 9/11 terrorist attacks. In the midst of the pandemonium, leaders of Reuters in New York City turned chaos into order by establishing a command center within half a day of the attacks.

Reuters had operations and employees in the World Trade Center as well as many other locations around the city. With a command center up and running, managers emerged every hour to give the staff updates. People in the top echelon pulled together as a team. Clear assignments were given. Priorities were established.

This was an extreme situation, but for any firm facing trouble, the lessons are obvious. I worked with one company that was in danger of shutting down because it was running out of operating capital. To establish order, lessen the anxiety and head off rumors, we set up a bulletin board for progress reports and held regular town-hall-style meetings with employees to address their questions and concerns.

The Playbook

- → As best as you can, make a plan and communicate it to everyone.

- → Gather your team, make assignments and establish priorities. Make sure everyone is clear about his or her responsibilities. Do the same with your family in a crisis.

- → Establish a situation room or command center to manage the flow of information.

- → Beware the rumor mill. Make sure you have a mechanism to counteract any false information that undoubtedly will begin to circulate. Use bulletin boards (electronic or otherwise) or hold town meetings to get out the word.

- → Be willing to make tough decisions, even if it means facing conflict.

- → Be honest. Be honest. Be honest.

Your Personal Playbook

Date:

Goal:

Motivation (why you are doing this):

Game Plan (how you will accomplish this):

Teammates (who will help):

Finish Line (when you will achieve this)

The Coach's Clipboard

Get the help you need

W e often don't hesitate to seek expert advice when we're trying to learn a skill like golf or cooking. Sometimes we seek out other experts—therapists or coaches—only when something feels broken. But sometimes we don't seek help at all because we are fearful or have feelings of shame.

Often when I work with clients who are having problems with someone on their staff, the real issue is that the other person hasn't taken care of his or her own problem. It may be that the person is depressed or anxious but not going to therapy. Or they may have anger management issues and aren't getting coaching for it. Perhaps their finances are a mess but they haven't sought outside help. Untreated addictions are another huge concern.

People in leadership positions then are stuck with having to confront people about whatever is causing the disruption. It's always better to tackle your own problems. The consequence of not doing so may be that you sink further into trouble.

The Playbook

→ If you think you have a psychiatric problem, seek therapy.

→ If you have a health problem, go to a doctor.

→ If you're having trouble managing your work role, go to a coach.

→ If you've got an addiction, go to a 12-step meeting or consult your physician.

→ If there's trouble on the home front, go to a family therapist or marriage counselor.

→ If you're having a spiritual crisis, seek out a clergy person.

→ If you're not sure what you should do, consult a friend or someone close to you.

→ Pray for guidance and remember the adage, "God helps those who help themselves."

Your Personal Playbook

Date:

Goal:

Motivation (why you are doing this):

Game Plan (how you will accomplish this):

Teammates (who will help):

Finish Line (when you will achieve this)

The Coach's Clipboard

Forget trying to control people

Leaders worry themselves to death over how to get people to do what they want them to do. In my book *Conversations with My Old Dog*, I write in a series of poems about the "talks" I used to have with my aging yellow lab Lucy. The poem titled *Control* includes these lines:

> *We people spend much of our time on the illusion*
> *of control—*
> *we order our lives and try*
> *to order the lives of others.*
> *However, we learn—as with our dogs—*
> *that we may get folks to sit*
> *but never to stay.*

I offer the same advice to the people I coach. It's difficult enough to control your own behavior; it's a losing proposition to try to control others'. Learn to appreciate their behavior instead.

The Playbook

→ No matter what your title, treat everyone with respect.

→ Take the time to engage people; ask questions and let them ask you questions. Give honest answers. Listen to their responses. It's better when you can hear from others what they think should be done. Collectively, you can try to control the outcomes.

→ Be willing to accept the mood and behavior swings of others. They, like you, are human.

→ Don't overestimate how well you know even the people closest to you—your spouse, your children, your parents. No matter how familiar you are with them, you cannot control them. Learn to enjoy the surprises rather than treating them as a sign of irrationality or rebellion.

→ Keep in mind that groups are even more complex than individuals. Appreciate the good things that can emerge when everyone feels empowered to speak.

→ Give yourself a pat on the back or make a note of the times when you manage to treat the behavior of others in a more positive way than you once would have.

→ Work at controlling the things you can control: Eat healthfully, exercise regularly and seek sources of inspiration to boost your emotional well being.

→ At best, you can only control one person: yourself.

Your Personal Playbook

Date:

Goal:

Motivation (why you are doing this):

Game Plan (how you will accomplish this):

Teammates (who will help):

Finish Line (when you will achieve this)

The Coach's Clipboard

Don't act just to maximize profits

Research continually shows that more money doesn't bring more happiness, and yet people continue to opt for money at the expense of less tangible things. We're driven by the capitalist philosophy to make decisions that maximize profits, but it isn't always best to choose that option— to work that extra day, forgo that vacation or skip your child's game or recital. Sometimes it's best to set aside the bottom line in favor of the memories and experiences it can help create.

When our sons were small, we tried to take an annual vacation to Hilton Head, even if we sometimes couldn't quite afford it. Years later, those memories were lodged among our most cherished.

More of us should take the time to consider what our money is buying—or not buying. It has been drummed into us, for example, that we need to save oodles in case we live to be 90, but what if we die at 62? What would we have given up to make money that we didn't live long enough to enjoy?

My friend Arlene's mother had Alzheimer's by the time she retired at 62. Arlene decided to take retirement as early as she could, even though it might cost her money in the long run.

The Playbook

→ Take that vacation (or do something else), even if it leaves a temporary hole in the budget. Memories are important, too.

→ Look around: Appreciate the things that you have that are not linked to money—your family, your friends, your neighbors.

→ Invest in relationships; they don't go up and down with the stock market.

→ Invest in your health.

→ Look around your business: Are you providing a good work experience for your staff? Don't just act to maximize your profits.

→ In down times, look for ways to preserve jobs, not cut them, by asking people to do with less or earn less until things turn around.

→ Take all of your vacation time.

Your Personal Playbook

Date:

Goal:

Motivation (why you are doing this):

Game Plan (how you will accomplish this):

Teammates (who will help):

Finish Line (when you will achieve this)

The Coach's Clipboard

Don't skimp on the feedback

35

S arah is a senior vice president at a company but sometimes still feels insecure about her work. When she was working on a big project that involved doing things she hadn't done before, she kept waiting for an acknowledgement from her boss. She started thinking she must be messing up because Jack had always been very good at giving her feedback and suddenly—nothing.

Finally, Sarah couldn't stand it any more and just asked Jack whether she was doing OK. To her surprise, Jack apologized for his own shortcoming in failing to offer feedback. "You're doing a great job and I'm just disappointed in myself that I'm the one who isn't doing a good job," he said. That cleared the air for both of them.

Some feedback is always better than no feedback.

The Playbook

- → Recognize that people are very sensitive to concern about where they stand. They'd rather know than have to guess. Give them at least one performance review a year. Two would be better.

- → People will read things into a leader's behavior. If you cancel a meeting or don't smile at someone in the hall, they may take it personally and it will begin to affect their performance. So, don't let it go too long. Say, "Sorry, I walked by you yesterday without acknowledging you. I was in the middle of thinking about something. I've been meaning to ask you how your son's surgery turned out."

- → Don't be afraid to give negative feedback. No feedback is worse than negative feedback.

- → Hold regular family meetings to exchange honest feedback on how each person is doing and feeling.

- → Don't leave your elected representatives out of the loop— give them your feedback, too. It may be the best way to push for change.

- → Give yourself some healthful feedback with an annual medical checkup.

Your Personal Playbook

Date:

Goal:

Motivation (why you are doing this):

Game Plan (how you will accomplish this):

Teammates (who will help):

Finish Line (when you will achieve this)

The Coach's Clipboard

Apologize when you're wrong

One year on vacation, when my wife and I were preparing for a doubles tennis match against our sons, I came out to the court after the boys to warm up. I asked Adam, who was 15 at the time, to move to the other end of the court, so I could hit to him and 11-year-old Daniel. But Adam balked. "Why don't you hit with Dan on your end, and I'll stay here on my end?" he said. That ticked me off, and when Dan sided with Adam, it ticked me off some more.

Though Adam reluctantly trudged to the other end, I was still irritated as I hit the first practice shot to him. He swung so hard that the ball flew right past me, close to my head. That did it. I threw down my racket, yelled some more and stomped off the court.

Adam did come and apologize a few minutes later, but he also complained about my rudeness. We played the set—which they won, of course—but later, after I'd had time to reflect, I also apologized to Adam.

"Dad," he said, "that's the first time I ever remember winning an argument with you."

I was startled by that, because I prided myself on being a fair and understanding dad.

"Yeah," Adam said, "but this is the first time you've admitted you were wrong without giving me a lecture about what I had done wrong."

The Playbook

→ Love does not mean never having to say you're sorry or wrong about something.

→ Leaders aren't more perfect than other people. Be strong enough to admit a mistake and set the record straight.

→ Don't try to hide your areas of vulnerability. Everyone has them.

→ Recognize when you are being domineering.

→ Talk it out with someone you have been upset with—the sooner, the better.

→ Learn to apologize without adding blame. ("I apologize ... but you provoked me.")

Your Personal Playbook

Date:

Goal:

Motivation (why you are doing this):

Game Plan (how you will accomplish this):

Teammates (who will help):

Finish Line (when you will achieve this)

The Coach's Clipboard

Don't be afraid to ask, "How am I doing?"

Truckers put it on the rear of their rigs—"How am I driving?"—but fear blocks many of us from asking for similar assessments of ourselves. The simple question—"How am I doing?"—can produce powerful revelations and the opportunity to change.

The best bosses I know gather their teams together regularly to seek feedback. They believe that if they ask for it about themselves, it will be easier for them to give it to others. They hold individual meetings with team members as well as group meetings to probe this question. Sometimes I act as a facilitator.

If people are reluctant to ask for feedback, it's usually because they fear something bad will come of it. And often, the people who most fear feedback have every reason to. While they may be adept at painting a positive picture of themselves to those above them, the view from below may not be so rosy—and they know it.

When they do get negative feedback, instead of asking, "What can I do about this?" they try to sidestep or downplay the issues. I've known leaders who deliberately avoided having some of the people under them fill out a questionnaire about their performance because they knew the answers would be negative.

If leaders don't ask the "How am I doing?" question, it's generally because they don't want to hear the answer. They know there's something negative there or they fear something will come out that will compromise them. The best leaders encourage honest give-and-take and recognize that technology has changed the equation. In the rough-and-tumble world of the Web and blogosphere, feedback is instantaneous and generally no-holds-barred.

The Playbook

→ Never criticize or challenge those who give you solicited feedback. You asked for it; now listen to it.

→ Follow up with the people who have given you feedback by telling them what actions you will take to address the points raised.

→ Try the "360 feedback" approach in which you get feedback from your supervisors, your peers and yourself.

→ Ask your kids and your mate for feedback.

→ Thank those who give you feedback.

Your Personal Playbook

Date:

Goal:

Motivation (why you are doing this):

Game Plan (how you will accomplish this):

Teammates (who will help):

Finish Line (when you will achieve this)

The Coach's Clipboard

Spread the credit

38

Richard Sheridan runs Menlo Innovations, a computer software development firm that has won awards for its flexible workplace concept. His teams work in pairs. Every week, the pairs switch around. This attacks a common problem in software development—where the software is so tied to one person, it's tough for anyone else to understand it or work with it.

Sheridan's idea was that if you have a lot of people on a project, you'll increase the brain power. People also will catch each other's mistakes more easily. And they'll continually look at the project with fresh eyes. In Sheridan's shop, it's not that no one gets the credit—it's that lots of folks get the credit.

One of the clients I'd been working with had an "Aha!" moment about sharing the credit after he'd driven a project through to success. When I complimented him on what a great job he'd done, he said, "It wasn't me. I just had a part in it." And he really meant it. I said, "Did you just hear what you said? You didn't take credit for it." And he said, "Yeah, I guess this is working!" And it was.

The Playbook

→ Try Sheridan's approach and have people work in small teams. Change up the composition of the teams every few weeks.

→ Give all the credit to the team, not to any single team leader or member.

→ Avoid blaming one person for a failure or setback. It's the team's responsibility, win or lose.

→ Work in a team yourself.

→ Send personal notes congratulating friends on their successes.

→ Celebrate family achievements, big and small, as a team.

Your Personal Playbook

Date:

Goal:

Motivation (why you are doing this):

Game Plan (how you will accomplish this):

Teammates (who will help):

Finish Line (when you will achieve this)

The Coach's Clipboard

Play hard

Nowadays play can mean doing something risky or adventurous. That appeals to folks who gravitate toward activities like motorcycle racing or sea kayaking. It's perfectly OK to let out your competitive or risk-taking urges in this way. In fact, sometimes it's the only way you can do it.

But you can play hard at more traditional endeavors as well. For some people, retreating to a getaway place to hike and fish, taking a cruise (shuffleboard can be a real killer!) or sitting on a beach serves the same purpose as motorcycle racing. I like to spend a few hours writing when I take a break from work. Golf also is a great way to bring the family together.

My mother-in-law, Jean, wanted to spend more time with my father-in-law, Ted, who loved to golf, so she took it up and really got into the game. The two of them started playing together, and the funny thing was that Jean got a hole-in-one early on but Ted had to wait until he was in his 80s. (In all, Jean has had four holes-in-one, but Ted has shot his age every year since he was 78.)

The Playbook

→ Find a hobby, activity or other endeavor that will separate you from your daily routine and replenish your energy and spirit.

→ Schedule some of your play time for activities with friends.

→ Plan a trip with your family.

→ Set up regular times to play with your kids. (And let them beat you in games.)

→ Take a daily walk with your significant other or take the day off to spend only with this person.

→ Don't work while on vacation; don't think about work when you're at play.

→ Join an adult sports league or activity group. Having fun in a group can lift your spirits.

→ Make a plan for the weekend ahead so everyone in the family is excited about it.

Your Personal Playbook

Date:

Goal:

Motivation (why you are doing this):

Game Plan (how you will accomplish this):

Teammates (who will help):

Finish Line (when you will achieve this)

The Coach's Clipboard

Manage your energy as well as your time

I hear people saying, "I don't have enough time." As Mary Martin, a business owner in Holland, Mich., says, often what they really mean is they don't have enough energy. As I coach, I first ask whether my clients feel engaged in their work. Then I ask about any family or health issues that may be preoccupying them. If there are some, I find out if there is any action they can take to resolve them. I also ask whether they are getting enough sleep, enough time at full rest and enough exercise.

Juan greatly improved his energy by taking a 20-minute walk/run with his new puppy every morning. Irene switched to a four-day workweek to be able to spend more time with her two young children. William sought a family therapist to help with problems with his son, who has attention deficit disorder. Alfred began taking his children to the golf course every Sunday for an outing. Josh went to a sleep disorder clinic to find out why his sleep was constantly disrupted.

These kinds of actions helped these leaders avoid the burnout that so often accompanies people in demanding roles. When you're a leader, you don't have to prove yourself with a superhuman effort or superhuman time commitment. Sustainability is more important. And to achieve that, you have to know what re-energizes you. It's all about discipline and knowing what recharges your batteries.

Managing time often is really about managing energy. It's not just becoming more efficient. People often will try to do two things at once—take calls in the car while driving home, for instance. But if the person previously used the drive home to unwind and recharge, now they're not giving themselves time for that. They're still working.

You really can't cheat time.

The Playbook

→ If you don't know what re-energizes you, ask the people around you. Ask your mate what he or she notices about your behavior—when you're up or down—and what led to it.

→ Keep an energy journal so you can zero in on when you lose your energy and when it's at a peak. Write in the journal what factors into your high-energy moments. Accept that you need these stimuli to boost your energy.

→ Ask yourself the questions I ask clients: Are you fully engaged in your work? Are there family or health problems that are preoccupying you? Can you take some action to resolve them? Are you getting enough sleep? Enough full rest? Enough exercise?

→ Take a nap.

→ Spend time on activities that give you a full sense of purpose.

→ Meditate.

→ Go to places that energize you, not to ones that drain your energy. (I write this as I sit in my local cupcake shop with many happy customers.)

Your Personal Playbook

Date:

Goal:

Motivation (why you are doing this):

The Playbook

→ Take time out from a difficult relationship if you need a cooling-off period, but let the person know that you'll be in touch at some point in the future.

→ Seek therapy if you feel it is warranted.

→ Take a look at your own behavior and how it may be contributing to the toxic interactions.

→ Bring in a mediator to work through the problem.

→ Keep in contact through written communications if nothing else.

Your Personal Playbook

Date:

Goal:

Motivation (why you are doing this):

Game Plan (how you will accomplish this):

Teammates (who will help):

Finish Line (when you will achieve this)

The Coach's Clipboard

Take good care of yourself

How many times have you heard people say it: If you don't have your health, you don't have anything. It may be a cliché, but it's true.

I was contacted by the owner of a small business, but the more we talked, the more it became clear that he was looking for more than business coaching. His work life was in pretty good shape, but he had just learned he might have a serious illness on top of ongoing health problems. Other family members also were battling illnesses. As soon as we began to talk, his health-related anxieties rose to the surface. He admitted that he was focusing so much on work because he didn't want to deal with these other worries.

Some research suggests that good economic times actually promote bad habits—people tend to drink too much, eat too much and slack off on exercise. Though the evidence is mixed about the opposite scenario—whether bad times can be good for you—it stands to reason that if you maintain good habits in good times, they'll be there for you when the tide turns.

The Playbook

- → Develop routines that promote good health: regular exercise, proper diet, self-reflection.

- → Get therapy if you can't get past a painful or traumatic point in life.

- → Curtail alcohol consumption. Meditate one night a week instead of having a beer or pouring a glass of wine.

- → Give up a bad habit. Make a plan, commit to it and be accountable to someone else.

- → Plan free days when you do no work.

- → Look in the mirror every day as a stimulus to lose weight.

- → Cook a healthful meal from scratch at least once a week.

- → Get a good night's sleep. Avoid caffeine before bedtime; watch what you eat and drink; avoid napping during the day; keep your bedroom quiet, cool, dark and well-ventilated; get regular exercise during the day.

- → Keep a personal journal where you make note of TGCOY (Take Good Care of Yourself) activities. Every day, I keep track in a notebook in my wallet an account of the good things that happen—something that I've done for others, something nice that was said to me and special things I've done for myself, including exercise. The daily repetition helps keep me accountable.

Your Personal Playbook

Date:

Goal:

Motivation (why you are doing this):

Game Plan (how you will accomplish this):

Teammates (who will help):

Finish Line (when you will achieve this)

The Coach's Clipboard

Be disciplined

Almost everyone I know who has achieved some degree of work-life balance has had to exert discipline. It doesn't always come naturally.

Mark, the CEO of a medical device company, tries to work his schedule to accommodate his job, his family and his church activities.

"I try to look at the balancing act over the course of the year as well as on a weekly basis," he says. "I make sure that … I have planned out time for significant events in each area. (The challenge is that work will be the one to eat from the other two if I allow it. So this is where I have to put limits on.)

"On the weekly time frame, I discipline myself to take advantage of the smaller opportunities with my family and church. Some of the items I actually schedule into my Outlook calendar at work so they do not get lost. Although managing my life's schedule purposefully and proactively can take the spontaneity out to some degree, it is better than not being there at all."

The Playbook

→ Use your calendar in whatever form to highlight important events (not just work-related ones) so that you can be sure you don't forget them.

→ If you have a good team at work, scheduling the other parts of your life will be a whole lot easier.

→ Don't fool yourself into thinking that nobody can make a contribution at work that's as good as yours. People who think this way try to do it all and inevitably end up being ineffective because they're tired, grumpy and burned out.

→ If you set up a healthy routine, stick with it for at least a few months.

Your Personal Playbook

Date:

Goal:

Motivation (why you are doing this):

Game Plan (how you will accomplish this):

Teammates (who will help):

Finish Line (when you will achieve this)

The Coach's Clipboard

Lighten up

Bill, who works for one of my bank clients, was about to go on medical leave for hip replacement surgery. He'd been in a lot of pain and was very nervous about the operation. But two of his coworkers—Amy and Lori—weren't about to let him go out the door without having a little fun—at his expense, of course.

They donned masks and latex gloves and wheeled in a make-believe hospital cart as if to prep Bill for surgery. There were lots of jokes and a special get-well kit. Everyone was in on it and gathered around to have a laugh and wish Bill well. It relieved everyone's tension and concern about Bill.

Workplaces are not sacred temples; they shouldn't be so buttoned-down that humor has no home.

The Playbook

→ As a leader, you set the tone. If you are gloomy, chances are your staff will be, too. If you can laugh, your staff will be more than happy to laugh with you.

→ If you squelch play at work, you risk stifling creativity.

→ Books have been written about the healing power of laughter. Cheer yourself up through laughter and bring a sense of humor to help others heal.

→ Families are funny—just think of the Simpsons, the Huxtables, Lucy and Desi. If you can't find humor in your family—and instigate some of it yourself—you're not trying hard enough.

→ Let yourself play at least a little every day. Find something that gives you that outlet. The spirit rejuvenates during play.

→ Friendship can be measured by the degree of humor you feel comfortable expressing. Spend time with people with whom you can share a laugh.

→ Accentuate the positive; say "Yes" as often as possible. Too often, leaders think their job is to say "No."

→ Even in your spiritual life, look for ways to express joy. Even Buddha laughs.

Your Personal Playbook

Date:

Goal:

Motivation (why you are doing this):

Game Plan (how you will accomplish this):

Teammates (who will help):

Finish Line (when you will achieve this)

The Coach's Clipboard

Build free days into your schedule

Bert Whitehead, a nationally known author and financial adviser based in Franklin, Mich., says he loses his creative juices without realizing it if he doesn't take time away from the job on a regular basis. And he doesn't just take time; he sets parameters. Here's how he describes it:

> "One of the most important things I have learned is that free days—taking off a series of 24-hour periods with **no** business intrusions (no phone calls, e-mail, reading, discussions, or even thinking about my business)—is critical to staying on the cutting edge. ... Free days have to be absolute. If I get a great idea and jot it down to work on later, that day is no longer a free day. In truth, I have never had a dearth of good ideas, and even if I forget this one, there are many more when I have rejuvenated myself."

Bert refers to these days as akin to saving money—if you don't do it "off the top" when your paycheck arrives, you may never do it. So Bert forces himself to schedule in these days first as he prepares his quarterly schedule.

"For best results," he says, "I make plane or other reservations for those free days so they don't get pre-empted later by pressing business."

The Playbook

→ Go into your calendar for the past year and calculate how many free days you've had. Now, sit down and figure out how many you want to take in the year ahead.

→ Mark your free days on your calendar ahead of time.

→ Plan a special trip with your family—one you can't easily get out of—and make the reservations so you're locked in.

→ On one of your free days, do a community service task that isn't in your regular routine and has nothing to do with your work.

→ Cut out one workday a week and turn it into a free day. Make this your "Sabbath."

→ On free days, treat your family and friends as well as you do your team. Schedule regular lunch or dinner dates with them to reconnect and catch up.

Your Personal Playbook

Date:

Goal:

Motivation (why you are doing this):

Game Plan (how you will accomplish this):

Teammates (who will help):

Finish Line (when you will achieve this)

The Coach's Clipboard

Be smarter than your smartphone

J ean-Jacques Rousseau said, "Man is born free, and
everywhere he is in chains." No kidding! Today's chains
often are digital: cell phones and computers.

Rick Reid, an account development manager for the Herman
Miller office furniture company, found one way to loosen the
shackles: Whenever he can, he parks his phone in the charger at
least one weekend day. It's his way of unchaining himself from
having to check e-mails and answer work-related calls. He wants
to be free to reconnect with his wife and children without having
to stay tuned to work.

You can do the same. All it takes is the ability to regularly
find the "off" button on your phone, your BlackBerry or your
laptop.

The Playbook

- → Set aside a day a week with your electronic buddies turned off.

- → You don't have to check your e-mail every minute of every day. Remove the imaginary seatbelt and step away from your computer at designated times.

- → Take a vacation where the cell phone towers won't reach.

- → Keep a journal about what it's like to be free.

- → Limit the number of times you check your e-mail each day.

- → Let people know that you will not be checking your e-mail or phone after a certain time each day.

- → Put your BlackBerry away when meeting with people or turn it off completely.

Your Personal Playbook

Date:

Goal:

Motivation (why you are doing this):

Game Plan (how you will accomplish this):

Teammates (who will help):

Finish Line (when you will achieve this)

The Coach's Clipboard

Do a strategic retreat with your family

C arrie and Steve both have high-powered jobs—Carrie in graphic design and Steve as a CFO. Steve wants to make a job change, but to find a job that pays as well, the family may have to move. They were conflicted about this and having trouble sorting everything out.

I suggested that they treat their family as a business enterprise and do a strategic retreat. Go away for a couple of days or sit down for a deep discussion, and examine what the costs of a job change—tangible and intangible—would be. I advised them to make a list of the things they each value, including elements such as:

- A good neighborhood for the kids.
- Someone to be home after school.
- Enough income to support their needs.
- A suitable place to worship nearby.
- Good health and retirement benefits.
- Jobs that allow everyone to be home for dinner most nights.

By talking through each item on their list, Steve and Carrie can come to a consensus about what the next step should be.

This process shifts the emphasis so all of the family's needs come into play, not just financial concerns.

The Playbook

→ Take your family as seriously as you do your business. Plan a strategic retreat to talk about where you stand, where you're headed, and how everyone is feeling.

→ Go away for a weekend or hire someone to coach you through the process.

→ Draw your children into the process. Get their opinions about how they would rank the various choices. For example, ask them if they would rather have mom and dad home every night or take an annual vacation to Disney World. The answer might surprise you.

Your Personal Playbook

Date:

Goal:

Motivation (why you are doing this):

Game Plan (how you will accomplish this):

Teammates (who will help):

Finish Line (when you will achieve this)

The Coach's Clipboard

Plan a weekly date night

Most leaders are careful about how they schedule their workdays, but many are far more casual about scheduling time with the people who mean the most to them. It's easy to fix, however, if you make it a point to set aside time every week to do something with your significant other.

Brad Labadie is in charge of football operations for the University of Michigan Wolverines. During the season, he never seems to have any free time, but during the off-season, he always plans a weekly date night with his wife, Melissa. Now that they have three children under age six, their date night often becomes a date morning, when they can at least get out for breakfast.

My wife, Pat, and I did something similar when our two boys were young. One morning a week when the kids were in school, we'd go out for breakfast at a favorite restaurant. We got to be such regulars, one of the waiters got to know us so well he started giving us advice on things like buying a house. Now that the children are grown, we've picked Wednesday night as our date night. We're both careful to adhere to keeping this time slot free.

Even newlyweds need this type of ritual. Jack and Emily, married only a few years, are working extremely hard on their careers. But they recognize the importance of togetherness. Monday night is their date night. Every week they pick the best movie in town and go to see it.

The Playbook

→ Set aside a regular time to be with your children as well as your significant other.

→ Make that regular time with your kids coincide with allowing your significant other to slip away for private time.

→ Don't leave your parents out of the loop. They'll get a kick out of knowing that you have set aside special time just to be one-on-one with them.

Your Personal Playbook

Date:

Goal:

Motivation (why you are doing this):

Game Plan (how you will accomplish this):

Teammates (who will help):

Finish Line (when you will achieve this)

The Coach's Clipboard

Learn to walk side by side

My wife and I have a favorite quote from Thomas Mann that we have framed in our bedroom:

Don't walk behind me, I may not want to lead.
Don't walk before me, I may not want to follow.
Walk by my side and let us be friends.

For us, it symbolizes the partnership aspect of our marriage. But in our fast-changing and troubled world, there's a good underlying message for everyone: We are all in this together. To take it a step further, it becomes even more important for us to bring our needs and wants into alignment—side by side— during unsettled times.

There is nothing like a worldwide financial meltdown to remind us that our reach may be exceeding our grasp. Is it time for Americans to re-evaluate, recalibrate? There's no question about that. Among other things, we have too much stuff, and, as the saying goes, the best stuff isn't stuff at all.

When my wife and I were in Rwanda conducting leadership training with the Ministers of Government, we noticed that many of the kids were wearing clothing that obviously had originated in the United States. They had repurposed many items—coats became dresses, for example. It drove home to us the point that we had lots of stuff moldering away in closets and dusty corners. When we got home, we cleaned house. We gave away anything that we could, because we realized other people needed it more than we did. But we benefited too, because we suddenly had a lot more room in our house.

Bill Gates, speaking about the foundation he established with his wife, said, "For Melinda and for me, the challenge is the same: How can we do the most good for the greatest number with the resources we have."

All of us have resources to share. All of us should look for ways to walk side by side with others.

The Playbook

→ Make recycling unused items a family project several times a year. Have each person go through their room or closet and make a pile of items to donate.

→ Turn dinnertime into a challenge to create a tasteful meal as economically as possible by using what is at hand.

→ Teach your children about giving by having them earn small amounts of money that they in turn donate to a special cause.

→ Instead of a big, expensive vacation, visit all those close-to-home destinations that you've forgotten about.

→ Get creative: Have each family member devise a fun outing that doesn't cost more than a few dollars or, better yet, nothing at all.

Your Personal Playbook

Date:

Goal:

Motivation (why you are doing this):

Game Plan (how you will accomplish this):

Teammates (who will help):

Finish Line (when you will achieve this)

The Coach's Clipboard

Send a message

Twenty-two years after graduating from high school, and after being appointed president of United Bank & Trust-Lenawee County, Joseph Williams was invited to give the commencement address at his alma mater in a small Michigan town. He chose to talk about the three things he believes contributed to his success:

- Develop your potential by consciously choosing the attitudes you display every day.

- Know your purpose in life. (Williams said his was to be "the best encourager on Earth.")

- Sow seeds that benefit others.

Of all the honors Joe received when he became bank president, none was more important than being asked to speak at the commencement. He took great pleasure in including in his speech a quote from psychologist William James:

> The greatest discovery of my generation is that human beings can alter their lives by altering their attitudes of mind.

Joe then encouraged the students to remember his mantra: "Choose your attitude every day."

The Playbook

→ Imagine you were asked to speak to the graduating class of your school. What message would you want to give?

→ Don't underestimate the value of a moment. You have the opportunity at any time to make a difference in the lives of those you encounter.

→ Remember where you came from, and to call Mom on Mother's Day and Dad on Father's Day. Thank them for your life and for their contributions to your success.

→ Choose your attitude every day.

Your Personal Playbook

Date:

Goal:

Motivation (why you are doing this):

Game Plan (how you will accomplish this):

Teammates (who will help):

Finish Line (when you will achieve this)

The Coach's Clipboard

Give back

"We are such spendthrifts with our lives," Paul Newman once told a reporter. "The trick of living is to slip on and off the planet with the least fuss you can muster. I'm not running for sainthood. I just happen to think that in life we need to be a little like the farmer who puts back into the soil what he takes out."

Who will really know why some succeed and some do not? Regardless of the circumstances, those who find themselves successful, whether by accident of birth or by their own hard work, fully distinguish themselves by giving back to the communities and societies from which they come.

To be a truly successful leader, you have to be like that farmer and put the seed back into the soil. Newman started camps for children with serious illnesses and began a food company that gave its profits to nonprofit organizations. He was a beacon for what successful leaders can do if they focus on giving back.

I am fortunate because I have met many leaders who are willing to give of themselves in appreciation for their success and in gratitude to society. Giving back has become more important to them than their initial success in business or industry.

They have started food-gathering organizations to collect the surplus from restaurants and give it to the hungry. They have rebuilt some of the worst parts of the worst cities in Michigan. They have gone to Africa to help governments treat AIDS. They have walked for breast cancer, adopted needy children and started projects to collect the stories of genocide survivors. They have helped the victims of Sept. 11 identify lost family members through DNA matching.

Even young people are giving back, often before they've even had time to earn an income or launch a career. My son Daniel, now in his late 20s, went to Thailand to help rebuild communities devastated by the 2004 tsunami. In his current role as a regional leasing associate with McKinley Inc. in Ann Arbor, Dan follows his company's policy of serving the community by actively participating as a board member of The Neutral Zone, a teen-run program in Ann Arbor. My cousin David, also in his 20s, has worked in Ethiopia to help children born with cleft palates. Numerous young adults worked on the 2008 presidential campaigns. All over America and throughout the world, people are making a difference by giving back.

The Playbook

- → Ask yourself: What am I doing today to give back?
- → As you become more successful, what is your dream about how to give back to society?
- → How will you plant the seeds today to replenish what you have been given in life?
- → How will you teach your children the importance of giving back?
- → What example are you setting for your children and coworkers about the importance of giving back?

Your Personal Playbook

Date:

Goal:

Motivation (why you are doing this):

Game Plan (how you will accomplish this):

Teammates (who will help):

Finish Line (when you will achieve this)

The Coach's Clipboard

Wake up from your deep sleep

I n my book *Awakening from the Deep Sleep,* I listed 25 examples of ways men can find themselves slumbering in the "deep sleep" of life. These largely were examples of what happens when traditional behaviors hold men back. My book was directed toward men, but the main message has a wider application: Anyone can be hemmed in by the expectations of others or of society as a whole.

I wrote *Awakening* because, in my practice as a psychologist, I met so many men who were so unhappy. I wanted to examine the challenges of growing up male in Western society and be an advocate for change. I feel the same way about the persistent gender-based expectations that constrain women and the race- and ethnicity-based ones that constrain people of color.

The 2008 presidential election vaulted these stereotypes onto the national stage once more. One can only hope that Barack Obama's election as the nation's first African-American president spurs further discussion and self-examination and helps to move everyone's sensitivity needle.

The Playbook

→ Connect with others in a meaningful, respectful manner.

→ Raise gender- and race-sensitive children. Let them know that it's OK with you that they don't conform to narrow stereotypes. Let them know that you expect them to treat everyone fairly and respectfully.

→ Everyone has negative scripts learned in childhood. Learn to recognize them—and then to change them.

→ Write down the areas where you think you need help with stereotyping. Talk about them with someone else.

→ Consider physician-essayist Lewis Thomas' words: "We are educated to be amazed by the infinite variety of life forms in nature; we are, I believe, only at the beginning of being flabbergasted by its unity."

→ Treat people the way you want to be treated.

→ Show respect to others; it may be the most important thing you can do.

→ Refrain from making racist or sexist statements and have the courage to challenge others when they make them.

Your Personal Playbook

Date:

Goal:

Motivation (why you are doing this):

Game Plan (how you will accomplish this):

Teammates (who will help):

Finish Line (when you will achieve this)

CHAPTER 6

You Be The Coach

The great thing about balanced leadership is that everyone ultimately gets to write their own script. As you work through issues, setting goals and formulating action plans, you will collect rich experiences and learn valuable lessons.

I meet regularly with CEOs and other business leaders to hear about the challenges they face and how they meet them. They never shy away from sharing their experiences in the hope that they might benefit others—and that others might return the favor.

I invite you to join the dialogue. I've established a Web site for aspiring leaders—RobsLeaders.info—where you will find a forum for exchanging ideas, information and expertise. Feel free to contribute your own Coach's Clipboard and Playbook ideas. Ask for advice or help. Share needs and wants.

RobsLeaders.info's most important job is to connect people.

And let me emphasize that my advice is not only for those well into their careers. Nothing would please me more than to reach much younger people and offer them the tools they will need to build their lives.

In recent times, with the American economy in turmoil, it has become too easy for people—especially young people— to throw up their hands and say that there are no more opportunities, no more chances to make a mark. But the history of our country—underscored anew by the inauguration of President Barack Obama—says otherwise, and the resiliency of the human spirit gives the lie to such negativity.

It's important to ask for what you want. You never know—the person on the receiving end of the request (perhaps even you!) may be in a position to grant your wish. Be bold, but be committed. Link up with those who will give you a positive message. There will always be a place, a job, a niche, for talented people.

Resources

Cameron, Kim. *Positive Leadership: Strategies for Extraordinary Performance.* San Francisco: Berrett-Koehler Publishers. 2008.

Collins, Jim. *Good to Great: Why Some Companies Make the Leap … and Others Don't.* New York: HarperCollins. 2001.

Dutton, Jane E., and Peter J. Frost, Monica C. Worline, Jacoba M. Lilius and Jason M. Kanov. "Leading in Times of Trauma." Harvard Business Review. January 2002.

Ellis, Albert, and Robert A. Harper. *A Guide to Rational Living.* Chatsworth, Calif.: Wilshire Book Co. 1997.

Fritz, Robert. *The Path of Least Resistance: Learning to Become the Creative Force in Your Own Life.* New York: Ballantine Books. 1989.

Goleman, Daniel; Richard Boyatzis and Annie McKee. *Primal Leadership: Learning to Lead with Emotional Intelligence.* Boston: Harvard Business School Press. 2004.

Gottman, John and Nan Silver. *The Seven Principles for Making Marriage Work.* New York: Three Rivers Press. 1999.

Isay, David. *Listening Is an Act of Love: A Celebration of American Life from the StoryCorps Project.* New York: Penguin Press. 2007.

Lakein, Alan. *How to Get Control of Your Time and Life*. New York: Signet. 1974.

New York Times. *Portraits: 9/11/01*. New York: Times Books. 2002.

Pasick, Robert. *Awakening from the Deep Sleep: A Powerful Guide for Courageous Men*. New York: HarperCollins. 1992.

Pasick, Robert. *Conversations with My Old Dog*. Canton, Mich.: David Crumm Media LLC. 2009.

Pausch, Randy with Jeffrey Zaslow. *The Last Lecture*. New York: Hyperion. 2008.

Quinn, Robert E. *Building the Bridge As You Walk On It: A Guide for Leading Change*. San Francisco: Jossey-Bass. 1996.

Quinn, Robert E. *Deep Change: Discovering the Leader Within*. San Francisco: Jossey-Bass. 1996.

Rath, Tom and Donald O. Clifton. *How Full Is Your Bucket? Positive Strategies for Work and Life*. New York: Gallup Press. 2004.

Wickman, Gino. *Traction: Get a Grip on Your Business*. Livonia, Mich. EOS. 2007.

Williamson, Marianne. *A Return to Love: Reflections on the Principles of a Course in Miracles*. New York: HarperCollins. 1992.

Robert Pasick holds a Ph.D. in psychology from Harvard University. For the past 30 years, as an organizational psychologist and executive coach, he has helped CEOs and their executive teams to profit during challenging circumstances. The author of five books, he has appeared on *The Oprah Winfrey Show*, *The Today Show* and *NPR*. Rob is president and founder of LeadersConnect and CEO Connect. As a faculty affiliate at the William Davidson Institute, Ross School of Business, University of Michigan, he has provided leadership training to the Ministers of Government of Rwanda

and to leaders in several other countries. Married for 39 years, and the father of two grown sons, Rob's roots are in both Detroit and New York City, and his heart is with family, friends, entrepreneurs, baseball and dogs, in that order.

contact: www.RobertPasick.com

⁓

Kathleen O'Gorman has been a newspaper editor with the Detroit Free Press, Louisville Courier-Journal and Ann Arbor News. She has bachelor's and master's degrees from the University of Michigan. Now a freelance writer and editor, she enjoys setting her own deadlines.

contact: kathyog@gmail.com

Colophon

This book was produced using methods that separate content from presentation. Doing so increases the flexibility and accessibility of the content and allows us to generate editions in different presentation formats quickly and easily.

The content is stored in a standard XML format called DocBook 5 (www.DocBook.org). Adobe InDesign®, the Oxygen® XML Editor and Microsoft Word® were used in the production.

- The print edition is set in Adobe Arno Pro type.
- Cover art and design by Rick Nease (www.RickNease.com).
- Editing by David Crumm.
- Copy editing and styling by Stephanie Fenton.
- Digital encoding and print layout by John Hile.

Printed in the United States
211901BV00004B/3/P

9 781934 879139